GEE MACRORY

LEARNING

TO TALK

THE MANY CONTEXTS OF CHILDREN'S LANGUAGE DEVELOPMENT

$SAGE

Los Angeles | London | New Delhi
Singapore | Washington DC | Melbourne

Los Angeles | London | New Delhi
Singapore | Washington DC | Melbourne

SAGE Publications Ltd
1 Oliver's Yard
55 City Road
London EC1Y 1SP

SAGE Publications Inc.
2455 Teller Road
Thousand Oaks, California 91320

SAGE Publications India Pvt Ltd
B 1/I 1 Mohan Cooperative Industrial Area
Mathura Road
New Delhi 110 044

SAGE Publications Asia-Pacific Pte Ltd
3 Church Street
#10-04 Samsung Hub
Singapore 049483

Editor: Amy Thornton
Senior project editor: Chris Marke
Marketing manager: Lorna Patkai
Cover design: Wendy Scott
Typeset by: C&M Digitals (P) Ltd, Chennai, India
Printed in the UK

Library of Congress Control Number: 2020949581

British Library Cataloguing in Publication data

A catalogue record for this book is available from
the British Library

ISBN 978-1-5264-8500-7
ISBN 978-1-5264-8499-4 (pbk)

At SAGE we take sustainability seriously. Most of our products are printed in the UK using responsibly sourced
papers and boards. When we print overseas we ensure sustainable papers are used as measured by the PREPS
grading system. We undertake an annual audit to monitor our sustainability.

LEARNING TO TALK

CONTENTS

ABOUT THE AUTHOR

Dr Gee Macrory is a former teacher and advisory teacher and was for many years a Principal Lecturer in the Faculty of Education, Manchester Metropolitan University, where she has extensive experience of teacher education in the field of primary and secondary modern foreign languages, bilingualism and early language development.

For Nina, Sasha, Jasmine, Ronnie and Jesse

PART I

INTRODUCTORY CONCEPTS

1

LEARNING TO TALK: HOW DO THEY DO IT?

Students of child development cannot fail to observe the remarkable progress that human infants make from the moment they are born. By the time they are two years old, generally speaking, they can boast of many accomplishments, including learning to sit, stand and walk, eat food, observe and engage with the world around them, and of course, learning how to talk. Consider this exchange between a mother and child, aged just two:

Mother: Tell Daddy we're playing in the sandpit.
Child: Look, Daddy, I'm playing in the sandpit.

At first glance, this may not seem particularly remarkable. But what has had to happen here for this exchange to be successful? First of all, the child has to discriminate between the different sounds of the language to understand the words that are being produced; she has to map the language onto concepts such 'play' and 'sandpit'; and she has to understand that she is being asked to relay this information to a third person. What she is able to do is attract her father's attention by use of the word 'look', and change the 'we're playing' to 'I'm playing', suggesting some kind of understanding (albeit unconscious) of how language has to be manipulated in order to convey meaning. On this occasion, of course, the words came out just right. However, any interaction with young children quickly reveals the myriad utterances that do not in fact come out just right! In the same week, this child also produced:

1. 'that's my one toe';
2. 'my come';
3. 'I'm wash my hands';
4. 'no roll it';
5. 'is daddy make the tea?';
6. 'daddy clean soap face'.

We typically find such utterances endearing and, at times, amusing. But they tell us much about the challenges that language – in this case, English – presents to the child seeking to master it. As adults, we use language with such facility that many of us are unaware of the sheer complexity of it. Furthermore, literacy is hugely influential in telling us where the word boundaries are, such that it is easy to forget that the young child has no such advantage and has the considerable task of figuring out what the words are from the stream of speech. The nearest most adults come to this is listening to people talking in a language they do not speak at all. Taking the examples above, we can of course only speculate about what is going on. With any of the examples shown, it is possible that all or some of each utterance is heard as one item. For example, 'my one' or 'roll it' may be perceived as one 'word' or item. The examples illustrate some of the things that have to be learned.

First, in example 1, we cannot have 'one' and 'toe' – one word has to be substituted for the other. However, somehow the child has to work out that 'my' and 'one' are separate words that can be used in different combinations. Yet, we could hypothesise that this has begun to happen as the child produces 'my come' (example 2), as this is unlikely to be something she has heard. The frequency of 'my' in the input (what the child hears) may be instrumental in what is available to her when she attempts to communicate. Learning that we say 'my' to refer to something we possess, but 'I' before a verb is a tricky business. In example 3, we can see that, in English, '-ing' is required as we can have 'I wash' but after 'I'm' we need 'washing'. The rules of negation in English are complex, so it is little wonder that in example 4 the child opts for a 'no' at the beginning of the utterance!

Equally, the rules that govern questions in English are also highly complicated, but of course many questions do indeed start with 'is' so example 5
appears to be a rather sensible move on the part of a two-year-old! In fact,
this particular two-year-old produced many questions starting with 'is'. I am
not, of course, suggesting any conscious strategy on the part of the child,
but pointing to one of the most commonly observed features of child language, namely the way in which they produce utterances that they clearly
have not heard. This suggests some creativity at work in their attempts to
communicate. Finally, in example 6, the utterance 'daddy clean soap face'
is quite typical of the way in which young children marshal the language
they have in pursuit of conveying meaning.

This brief look at a two-year-old needs also to be considered within the
context of where she has come from and where she is travelling to. Only
ten months earlier, at the age of fourteen months, the same child had a
repertoire of ten items that could be described as a 'word'. Scroll forward
three years or so and the utterances are noticeably more sophisticated, such
as 'I want to find a clean picture that hasn't been coloured in yet' and
'because we should have been having grown up dinner tonight, can I stay
up late?' Yet, as we shall see in later chapters, there is still much to learn,
as illustrated by such utterances as 'that's what I've been teached, not to fall
it out' and 'this is uncomfortabling me'.

So far, I have hinted at a number of issues that are highly pertinent to the
study of child language development. One is the task facing the child who
has to somehow decipher the stream of speech, and understand what she
is hearing, which perhaps raises the question as to what her interlocutors
are doing that might facilitate this. Another issue which I have alluded to is
the creativity of children, who regularly produce utterances that they clearly
have not heard in the input. The other issue that has been raised by the
preceding section is that of progress and development over time. A pressing
concern, particularly among early years' practitioners, is knowing what is to
be expected and when.

In the UK, recent reports have alerted practitioners to possible problems,
indicating that children are arriving at school without age-appropriate language skills. The *Bercow Report* of 2008 reminded us that communication
is a fundamental human right and a key life skill, and stated that approximately 50 per cent of children and young people in some socio-economically
disadvantaged populations have speech and language skills that are significantly lower than those of other children of the same age. Furthermore,
approximately 7 per cent of five year olds entering school in England –
nearly 40,000 children in 2007 – had significant difficulties with speech and/
or language (Bercow, 2008: 13–14).

In the same year, the Smith report (Gross, 2008) stressed the importance
of getting in early. Gross argued for intervention with four- to eight-year-
olds, suggesting that:

remedial action even at eight, nine or 10 is too late – given that a child failing to achieve the nationally expected standard at age seven in reading, writing and maths has an almost zero chance of later getting five good GCSEs (General Certificate of Secondary Education, taken at age 16 in the UK), including English and maths, compared with a 46% chance for a seven-year-old achieving the standard in all three areas and 10% for one achieving it in just one area.

(2008: 18)

This is reiterated by a recent report from the charity Save the Children (2018), arguing that the most important factor in reaching the expected levels in English and Mathematics at seven was children's language skills at age five, which they found to be greater than the link to poverty or poor parental education. Compared with their peers, children who struggled with language skills at age five were significantly less likely to reach the expected standards in English and Mathematics, regardless of family background, while children who struggled with language skills at age five scored on average 34 per cent worse in English and 26 per cent worse in Mathematics at age seven than children who had been at the expected level at age five. A Newcastle University report for the Early Intervention Foundation (Law *et al.*, 2017), however, reports that 5–8 per cent of all children in England and Wales are likely to have language difficulties, but that children from socially disadvantaged families are more than twice as likely to be diagnosed with a language problem. They note that, in the UK, approximately 85,000–90,000 children between the ages of two and six are referred to speech and language therapists each year, and 18–31 per cent of children aged 19–21 months living in disadvantaged communities have been found to have language delay that warrants referral for specialist assessment (Law *et al.*, 2017: 7).

Roulstone *et al.* (2011) stress the vital importance of the first 24 months; their findings suggested that children's understanding and use of vocabulary and two–three word utterances at 24 months was very strongly associated with their school readiness at age four to five, even when adjusted for social class. They found a strong relationship between the elements of the child's communication environment (such as the number of books available) and their ability to use words at 24 months. A follow-up report in 2018 to the 2008 *Bercow Report* suggested that more than 10 per cent of all children and young people, over 1.4 million in the UK, have long-term speech, language and communication needs (SLCN) which create barriers to communication or learning in everyday life: of these, 7.6 per cent have developmental language disorder and 2.3 per cent have language disorders associated with another condition such as autism or hearing impairment. SLCN includes conditions such as speech difficulties, stammering and many others. The report also affirms the crucial role of communication, but notes that there is insufficient awareness of children and young people's speech, and that there is far too much variation in the support children and young people receive for their SLCN. Furthermore, it emphasises how important it is that people working with children and young people with SLCN must have the skills and knowledge needed to confidently identify and support them.

Thus there can be little doubt that a sound grasp of what typical development looks like can only serve to support appropriate intervention on the part of early years' practitioners and primary school teachers. I should also add that, while in this introductory section we have concentrated upon language, we must also take into account the role of cognitive, social and emotional development.

The importance of description of children's language cannot be overestimated. Indeed, Ingram (1989) suggests that the twin goals for language development researchers are description and explanation. What do children say and how do they come to speak like this? What description does is furnish us with data for analysis, although we will see that different theoretical perspectives do not all accord the same importance to the data. Furthermore, different theoretical perspectives accord different weighting to such things as children's innate capacities, their social, cognitive and emotional development and the role of the input. All those involved with the teaching and care of children will find in the differing explanations implications for the ways in which they interact with them. This chapter will now focus on the different theories that have been put forward to explain how children learn language. We are considering here the concept of monolingual development, but we will consider bi- and plurilingual development in Chapters 5 and 6, as of course the majority of the world's babies grow up speaking more than one language.

THEORETICAL PERSPECTIVES

First of all, research into how children learn language is no new phenomenon. Saxton (2017: 283) tells us that the earliest systematic study of child language was reported by Tiedemann in 1787. According to Ingram (1989), the periods 1876–1926 and 1926–57 were characterised respectively by diary studies and large sample studies. However, it is generally agreed that it is the last 50 or so years which have seen a real upsurge of research in this area. What happened?

In the 1950s and 1960s, our understanding of children's language was influenced by work in **behaviourist** psychology. Behaviourist approaches are predicated on the idea that certain responses can become associated to stimuli in the environment, famously illustrated by the experiment commonly known as 'Pavlov's dogs', published in 1897. In this experiment, dogs were summoned to eat by a bell. Gradually, however, the dogs began to salivate at the sound of the bell, not the food. This is known as 'classical conditioning' and became the foundation of the school of behaviourist psychology, arising in the late 19th century. Together with the concept of operant conditioning, which proposes that the strength of a behaviour is modified by reinforcement or punishment, this became very dominant in the mid-20th century (Harley, 1995). How did this affect our conceptions of how language is learned? This is perhaps best summed up by the title of behaviourist psychologist B.F. Skinner's (1957) book on language, called *Verbal Behavior*. According to Skinner, language was just another kind of behaviour. He took the view that children were essentially products of their environment, with their speaking skills developed by the processes of imitation, reinforcement and gradual approximation of the target language. In this perspective, children imitate their parents or caregivers, who in turn reinforce and 'train' their children to perform in particular ways. Indeed, we have probably all observed something akin to this in action, perhaps, for example, when parents say something like 'say thank you', and praise the child for the correct response. Later this may take the shape of a question such as 'what do you say?', prompting the child to recall and produce the correct phrase. Similarly, children may be coaxed into copying new words and practising their pronunciation.

At this stage, you may already be wondering about some of the utterances we looked at earlier in this chapter. Who could have trained a child to say 'my come'? So, while we may all have observed some elements of parental or caregiver interaction that could be considered behaviourist in approach, it seems that this cannot be the whole story. Noam Chomsky certainly did not think so. The publication of Skinner's book sparked a major reaction that resulted in a real tension in the field of child language. Chomsky in a review of the book (1959) highlighted what he saw to be major flaws with Skinner's case. A key observation was that children must do more than imitate: as we have already seen, children say things that they have never heard before, which suggests that their language is *creative*. A further aspect is that their language tends to be rule-governed and systematic. An oft-quoted experiment by Jean Berko (1958) has frequently been used to illustrate this: young children were shown pictures of a bird-like creature called a 'wug'. When shown two of these, they called them 'wugs', suggesting that they were aware of the rule about plural 's' in English. Similar behaviour is easily observable in young children, as they, for example, over-generalise the past tense ending '-ed' to produce such utterances as 'goed'. Other characteristics of child language include the fact that all children go through developmental stages. For example, we know that children will acquire their first words at approximately a year old and combine these around 18–24 months of age. What is also interesting is the cross-language similarity – so when the English baby is saying 'more milk', the German baby is saying 'mehr Milch' (Slobin, 1971: 44), suggesting that there is more to language acquisition than responding to the environment. Another point that appeared to play down the role of the environment was the apparent resistance to correction that young children have, and the literature abounds with examples of parents' failed attempts to correct their young children's language. Finally, Chomsky noted the speed of acquisition, and indeed we have observed earlier in this chapter the impressive progress that young children make in a relatively short space of time.

These factors led Chomsky to conclude that children must be born with a **language acquisition device** (LAD), an innate component that is assumed to be a specialised part of the brain. While this component requires input from the environment to trigger it, the role of the environment is notably downplayed in comparison to a behaviourist approach. Pinker (1994) argues that language develops in children spontaneously, without conscious effort or formal instruction, and is distinct from more general abilities to process information or behave intelligently. He asserts that 'people know how to talk in more or less the sense that spiders know how to spin webs' (1994: 18).

This debate between Chomsky and Skinner had other ramifications, however. At this stage, linguists (as opposed to psychologists) had only just begun to consider child language acquisition as a legitimate domain of enquiry. At the time, mid-century, linguists were primarily interested in the structure of language as an independent system of rules – that is, an assumption that language has a structure of grammar that is somewhat independent of language use. A grammar is a finite set of rules that can generate an infinite number of permissible sentences, allowing adult speakers of a language to produce and understand utterances they have never heard or said before. Leopold, a linguist, had in 1949, through a descriptive account of his own children's language development, made the case that 'the study of child language is definitely a concern of general linguistics' (1949: 10). Chomsky's arguments that there existed a LAD turned the field away from data-driven approaches and towards a more theory-driven, mentalist approach, creating a tension that still exists. Chomsky's approach is often referred to as nativist, implying the existence of an innate module that the child is said to be born with. Some support for this idea also came from a perspective that there was a biological basis to language development. Lenneberg (1967), following Penfield (1965), proposed that there was a 'critical period' for language acquisition, which led to the CPH (critical period hypothesis). This suggested that there was a finite period when language could be acquired, ending at puberty, although subsequently it has been suggested that if there is a 'cut-off' point, this could be much younger, such as five years of age (Krashen, 1973). Unsurprisingly, this notion has been of interest to researchers in the field of second-language acquisition (see, for example, Birdsong, 2013). We will look at this issue further in Chapter 6. A final thing to note for now, however, is that the Chomskyan approach tended to highlight the place of *grammar* in language acquisition.

There were soon some counter-arguments to Chomsky's ideas. Challenges to his grammar-focused perspective came first from those that argued for a semantic basis to children's language (e.g. Bowerman, 1973). Instead of looking at children's utterances in terms of their grammatical construction, the role of **meaning** (semantics) was highlighted. If we take, for example, an utterance like 'daddy car', this can be described grammatically as noun + noun; alternatively we can speculate as to what *meaning* the child is seeking to convey, which could be the equivalent of the adult 'daddy is in the car', 'daddy please take me in the car', 'daddy's car' and so on. The emphasis on seeking meaning in child language also reflects a concern with cognitive development and its relationship with language. Piaget (1926) is possibly one of the most well-known writers on child development: like Chomsky, he believed that innate abilities were responsible for development; unlike Chomsky, he did not believe that there was a separate 'module' in the brain governing language acquisition. Rather, general cognitive abilities lay underneath the acquisition of language: language depends on thought for its development (see Harris and Butterworth, 2002). His constructivist approach emphasised the agency of young children, who are seen as active learners, engaged with their world (Donaldson, 1978; Halpenny and Pettersen, 2014). Children began to be seen as 'meaning makers' (Halliday, 1975; Wells, 1986). Once conceived of as this, it is not hard to understand why researchers became interested in their behaviour as conversationalists, constructing meaning in conversation with other language users. This interest was focused initially on the input the child received and later the interaction she engaged in. With regard to the input, Chomsky's argument was that the input was degenerate, too impoverished to facilitate language acquisition (1965). This was challenged by those who observed the particular nature of speech addressed to children, initially dubbed 'motherese' (Newport *et al.*, 1977: 112) and later amended to the more inclusive or neutral '**child directed speech**' (CDS). Challenging the idea that the input was impoverished, a number of researchers pointed out several characteristics of the speech children were exposed to. First, it seemed that the speech addressed to children was higher in pitch and with exaggerated intonation patterns. Lay observers might perceive this as a 'sing song' type of intonation and many of us will have noticed this when listening to adults talking to young children (and often to pets too!). Research has also shown that parents and caregivers tend to stick to age-appropriate topics, vocabulary relevant to the young child and a limited range of grammatical structures. A very influential volume by Snow and Ferguson (1977) was notably entitled *Talking to Children*, and this included examples from different cross-cultural contexts, such as Latvia, Morocco and Kenya. Charles Ferguson, in the same volume, describes 'baby talk' (BT) as a simplified register, but suggests, however, that the simplifying processes used in BT are not universal in the sense that they all occur in all languages

(1977: 216). Indeed, some researchers such as Heath (1983) and Lieven (1994) have challenged the idea that this register of speech directed to children is a world-wide one, citing examples of other cultures where the approach to conversing with children is somewhat different. For example, Lieven notes a number of studies that report an absence of speech addressed to prelinguistic children (1994: 59). More recently, however, Saxton (2017: 112) concluded that the majority of children in the world are exposed to some aspects of CDS, although he argues that this facilitates language acquisition rather than being wholly necessary.

Attention began to shift in the direction of the interactions in which children were engaged, resulting in what became known as **interactionist** approaches. We have already noted Piaget's view of the importance of cognition and its relationship with language. He is, however, seen by some as adopting an interactionist perspective as he took the view that the complex structures of language might be neither innate nor learned. Rather, they emerged as a result of the interaction between the child's current cognitive capacities and the linguistic and non-linguistic environment. For example, it is only when a child arrives at the stage of 'object permanence' that a word is needed. In other words, around the end of the first year of life, infants come to understand that an object still exists if she cannot see it. Prior to this, once an object has disappeared, it essentially ceases to exist for the child (Bohannon and Bonvillian, 2001: 276–7). But once the child has a mental representation of something, then a symbol to represent it is needed – and words function as symbols. Put simply, if you now know that your juice still exists somewhere, it needs a name if you are going to summon it up!

There are, of course, other ways to conceive of interaction. Importantly, the role of **social context** was highlighted by a number of researchers. The social interactionist approach emphasises the role of the environment, but, unlike the earlier behaviourist explanations, in this scenario, the child is no passive recipient of language. This perspective recognises the language is learned and used for social purposes. We use language to communicate meanings to *other people* and to understand and respond to the things they wish to convey to us. But conveying concepts and ideas using grammar and vocabulary is nowhere near the whole story. The social context affects the choice we make of vocabulary and grammatical structures, and often these are 'embedded' in a social situation. On one level, this can be explained by register ('would you mind handing me that pen?' vs 'Give me that pen!'), but, equally, before they are introduced to these social nuances, young children's interactions are often anchored in a social context that allows them to make sense of the input and gain responses to their own utterances. So, for example, the familiar context of bath time may facilitate the relevance of what the parent is saying, as that parent makes reference to familiar objects and activities. Furthermore, within that context, children can take the lead in choosing what to refer to and what to talk about, and social interactionists hold that young children talk with intent – a far cry from the passive child implied by the behavourist account. But the child may then also elicit from the parent or caregiver repetitions of pronunciation, expanded responses (both in terms of the grammar and the vocabulary used) and recasts (which are essentially reformulations of the child's utterance in a grammatically correct way). In this view, the child and adult are engaged in a dynamic exchange that enables the child not only to attach cognitive or semantic concepts to the language, but also to begin to appreciate that language is a social and communicative tool, while hearing repeated examples of the language used appropriately and in context.

This approach owes something to the work of Russian psychologist, Vygotsky, whose work was originally published in Russia in 1934 and only in 1962 in English. His work has proved to be hugely influential in the field of education more generally, but his influence on our understanding of language development is also important. In contrast to Piaget, for Vygotsky, cognitive development results from an internalisation of language. Vygotsky's work very much placed the responsibility for human development on the social environment. His approach is social-constructivist and his notion of 'scaffolding' learning affords a key role to more mature others in the environment, emphasising the role of communication, social interaction and instruction on determining the path of human development (Wood, 1998: 37). In terms of language development, this emphasis on interaction is reflected in the volume entitled *Input and Interaction in Language Acquisition* (Gallaway and Richards, 1994), seen as a sequel to the earlier volume by Snow and Ferguson (1977) mentioned above. The book by Gallaway and Richards signalled a real shift towards interaction as well as input, and the collection featured a range of contexts including other family members and atypical learning situations (for example, hearing impairment), as well as school settings in addition to home ones.

The focus on the *context* of language learning along with technological approaches over the last nearly 30 years has also been instrumental in the development of other challenges to the nativist (Chomskyan) perspective. Although, as we have seen, researchers were able to point to evidence that the input was not, in fact, degenerate, demonstrating precisely *how* young children somehow inferred the rules of their language from this input remained, if not exactly a mystery, a still unexplained phenomenon. The work of Tomasello and colleagues from the early 1990s on, however, began to address this issue. This perspective comes within the field of what is known as cognitive linguistics, and is also known as a **usage-based approach**, which takes the view that children's language development is essentially cognitive in nature. In this view, linguistic structures arise from cognitive schemas similar to those that exist in other cognitive domains, because recurrent events are characterised by recurrent communicative roles. Put simply, children learn – subconsciously – to associate certain language with particular events, the structure or routine of which is familiar and even predictable, such as the language likely to be produced at bath time or meal time. Saxton (2017: 279) suggested recently that this perspective has emerged over the last ten years as the most viable alternative to the nativist paradigm. Tomasello's seminal work in 1992, *First Verbs*, a diary study of his own infant daughter, noted that children's early utterances were not always what they seemed (Tomasello, 1992). What he observed was that certain forms of the same verb were used in quite different contexts, allowing him to conclude that, for example, the words 'made' and 'make' were for his young daughter not related in any way. This is a very different interpretation from a traditional conclusion that she had acquired a 'past tense'. This led him to formulate the 'verb island hypothesis', which held that verbs gradually expanded the range of contexts in which they were used, so that the child over time built up sufficient representations to permit some abstract categories to emerge (subconsciously, of course) in her mind. Rather than this being innate, he argues that children are making generalisations based on the input they receive, from which they subsequently form these abstract categories. In my own diary study (see Macrory, 2001) I noted that when 'should have' first appeared, the first few times were with 'put' as in 'should have put'. Gradually, over time, other items replaced 'put', suggesting that, first, 'should have put' had simply been learned as an unanalysed utterance and, second, that it takes time for the child's brain to analyse the input, break it down and start producing new combinations. Thus, what is an apparently sophisticated utterance is much less assured than it seems. But the language does, of course, become increasingly secure: Tomasello also noted the way in which new utterances recycled and expanded language previously learned (Macrory, 2001: 28). Tomasello's insights build on earlier research in both first- and second-language acquisition that children often use unanalysed routines in their production that can create an air of sophistication, and at times cause amusement because they are clearly too 'adult' in their expression. I can recall the sense of amusement – even bemusement – when my two-year-old daughter, after eating, said 'thank you for my lunch'. Only when this was quickly followed by 'come on Jess' did I realise that the whole utterance was mimicking a scene from a popular children's programme called *Postman Pat* that featured not only the postman but his cat, Jess! This illustrates the way in which children do possess a sophisticated ability to understand event structures (Snow, 1999: 261) – if you like, the routines of everyday life – which allows them to 'map' meaning on to experience, but also somehow to infer and use the grammatical constructions that link language and events, gradually adding to these and expanding their scope. Important in this perspective is what is known as theory of mind – that is, the ability to attribute mental states such as beliefs, intents, desires and so on to oneself and to other people, necessary to understanding that others have beliefs, desires, intentions and perspectives that are different from one's own. According to this view, children have an impressive ability to figure out these event structures *and* to understand the intentions of adults as expressed through language, while also possessing a sophisticated capacity for imitative learning (Tomasello, 2001, 2003). Of course, children's ability to extract unanalysed routines may go unnoticed at times, if the utterance is correct in the adult language. It would not be immediately obvious, for example, that 'what's that?' might have been learned as an unanalysed utterance.

However, there is a need to demonstrate that there is, in fact, some kind of relationship between the language that children hear and engage with and the language they themselves produce.

Technological advances have greatly facilitated the ability of researchers to document and quantify the language that young children produce as well the language that they hear. While tape recorders were available and used many years ago, the advent of computer technology and software programs has allowed us to not simply record, but also to quantify the frequency of items in the child's repertoire and in the parents' or caregivers'. The Language ENvironment Analysis (LENA) system recently offered a new tool (LENA Research Foundation, 2014), a device that parents can use to easily monitor the amount of language stimulation their child receives. The LENA device is a small, child-safe recorder that children wear for a day at a time. Much more long-standing is the Child Language Data Exchange System (CHILDES, MacWhinney, 1991), which also has software called computerized language analysis (CLAN) which allows automated analyses such as word searches and frequency counts. Studies using this kind of analysis show correlations between input and output, so that, for example, in a study of the development of question forms in a young French–English bilingual child, I was able to show that my subject, Adèle, appeared to use the language she most frequently heard (Macrory, 2007). At one level, this is hardly surprising. There has to be an element of imitation – after all, French-speaking parents have French-speaking children, Mandarin-speaking parents have Mandarin-speaking children and so on. As we have seen, children do copy the input but they also possess the capacity to produce novel utterances and items that they clearly have not heard. At this point, you may feel we are back to where we started – the behaviourist argument versus Chomsky's challenge. However, research in the intervening years has revealed a picture that is complex and intriguing, one where research has significantly developed our understanding of young children's cognitive and communicative capacities, and of their ability to discern the relationships between language and events in the world and make use of this to generate their own utterances and infer patterns and rules. This has led us to have a much more nuanced understanding of the role that imitation plays in language development, and the potential contribution of interaction with parents and caregivers.

CHAPTER SUMMARY

We have in this chapter provided a brief historical overview of explanations for how young children acquire a first language. We have seen how over the last half-century explanations of language development have become much nuanced, as they have had to take into account research findings pertaining to cognitive development, input *and* interaction, and the findings from a usage-based approach that suggest that young children have a sophisticated ability to discern pattern in language and relate this to the context in which they hear it. This points to a major role for input and interaction, challenging the nativist position and the idea of some language acquisition device. If this is the case, then there are clear implications for parents and caregivers, in that the context they provide is crucial to the children's language development. The contexts of language acquisition and development that pertain, are, however, highly variable, as we will see in later chapters of this book.

REFERENCES

Berko, J. (1958) The child's learning of English morphology. *Word*, 14, 150–77.

Birdsong, D. (ed.) (2013) *Second Language Acquisition and the Critical Period Hypothesis*. London: Routledge.

Bercow, J. (2008) *The Bercow Report: A Review of Services for Children and Young People (0–19) with Speech, Language and Communication Needs*. London: Department for Children, Schools and Families.

Bercow, J. (2018) *Bercow: Ten Years On. An Independent Review of Provision for Children and Young People with Speech, Language and Communication Needs in England*. London: Department for Children, Schools and Families.

Bohannon, J.N. and Bonvillian, J.D. (2001) Theoretical approaches to language acquisition. In Gleason, J.B. (ed.), *The Development of Language*. 5th edn. London: Allyn and Bacon.

Bowerman, M. (1973) Structural relationships in children's utterances: syntactic or semantic? In T. Moore (ed.), *Cognitive Development and the Acquisition of Language*. New York: Academic Press.

Chomsky, N. (1959) Review of *Verbal Behavior*, by B.F. Skinner. *Language*, 35, 26–58.

Chomsky, N. (1965) *Aspects of a Theory of Syntax*. Cambridge, MA: MIT Press.

Donaldson, M. (1978) *Children's Minds*. London: Fontana.

Gallaway, C. and Richards, B.J. (eds) (1994) *Input and Interaction in Language Acquisition*. Cambridge: Cambridge University Press.

Gross, J. (2008) (ed.) *Getting in Early: Primary Schools and Intervention*. London: Smith Institute.

Halliday, M.A.K. (1975) *Learning How to Mean: Explorations in the Development of Language*. London: Edward Arnold.

Halpenny, A.M. and Pettersen, J. (2014) *Introducing Piaget*. E-book. New York: Routledge.

Harley, T.A. (1995) *The Psychology of Language: From Data to Theory.* Hove: Erlbaum.

Harris, M. and Butterworth, G. (2002) *Developmental Psychology: A Student's Handbook.* London: Psychology Press.

Heath, S.B. (1983) *Ways with Words: Language, Life and Work in Communities and Classrooms.* Cambridge: Cambridge University Press.

Ingram, D. (1989) *First Language Acquisition: Method, Description and Explanation.* Cambridge: Cambridge University Press.

Krashen, S. (1973) Lateralization, language learning and the critical period: some new evidence. *Language Learning,* 23, 63–74.

Law, J., Charlton, J. and Asmussen, K. (2017) *Child Language as a Wellbeing Indicator.* London: Early Intervention Foundation.

LENA Research Foundation (2014) *The LENA Research Foundation.* Available at: http://www.lenafoundation.org/ (accessed 25 August 2020).

Lenneberg, E. (1967) *The Biological Foundations of Language.* New York: Wiley.

Leopold, W.F. (1949) *Speech Development of a Bilingual Child: A Linguist's Record. Vol III. Grammar and General Problems in the First Two Years.* New York: AMS Press.

Lieven, E.V.M. (1994) Cross-linguistic and cross-cultural aspects of language addressed to children. In C. Gallaway and B.J. Richards (eds), *Input and Interaction in Language Acquisition.* Cambridge: Cambridge University Press.

Macrory, G. (2001) Language development: what do early years practitioners need to know? *Early Years: An International Journal of Research and Development,* 21(1), 33–40.

Macrory, G. (2007) Constructing language: evidence from a French–English bilingual child. *Early Child Development and Care,* 177(6), 781–92.

MacWhinney, B. (1991) *The CHILDES Project: Tools for Analyzing Talk.* Hillsdale, NJ: Lawrence Erlbaum.

Newport, E., Gleitman, H. and Gleitman, L.R. (1977) Mother, I'd rather do it myself: some effects and non-effects of maternal speech style. In C.E. Snow and C.A. Ferguson (eds), *Talking to Children: Language Input and Acquisition.* Cambridge: Cambridge University Press.

Penfield, W. (1965) Conditioning the uncommitted cortex for language learning. *Brain,* 88, 787–98.

Piaget, J. (1926) *The Language and Thought of the Child.* San Diego, CA: Harcourt, Brace.

Pinker, S. (1994) *The Language Instinct.* London: Penguin.

Roulstone, S., Law, J., Rush, R., Clegg, J. and Peters, T. (2011) Investigating the role of language in children's early educational outcomes. *Research Report DFE-RR134.* London: Department for Education.

Save the Children (2018) *Early Language Development and Children's Primary School Attainment in English and Maths: New Research Findings.* Available at: https://resourcecentre.savethechildren.net/library/early-language-development-and-childrens-primary-school-attainment-english-and-maths-new-0 (accessed 20 June 2020).

Saxton, M. (2017) *Child Language.* 2nd edn. London: SAGE.

Skinner, B.F. (1957) *Verbal Behavior.* Acton, MA: Copley.

Slobin, D. (1971) *Psycholinguistics.* London: Scott, Foresman and Co.

Snow, C.E. (1999) Social perspectives on the emergence of language. In B. MacWhinney (ed.), *The Emergence of Language*. Hillsdale, NJ: Lawrence Erlbaum.

Snow, C.E. and Ferguson, C.A. (1977) (eds) *Talking to Children: Language Input and Acquisition*. Cambridge: Cambridge University Press.

Tomasello, M. (1992) *First Verbs: A Case Study of Grammatical Development*. Cambridge: Cambridge University Press.

Tomasello, M. (2001) Perceiving intentions and learning words in the second year of life. In M. Bowerman and S.C. Levinson (eds), *Language Acquisition and Conceptual Development*. Cambridge: Cambridge University Press.

Tomasello, M. (2003) *Constructing a Language: A Usage-Based Theory of Child Language Acquisition*. Cambridge, MA: Harvard University Press.

Vygotsky, L. (1962) *Thought and Language*. Cambridge, MA: MIT Press.

Wells, G. (1986) *The Meaning Makers: Children Learning Language and Using Language to Learn*. Portsmouth, NH: Heinemann.

Wood, D. (1998) *How Children Think and Learn*. 2nd edn. Oxford: Blackwell.

2

TALKING ABOUT TALK

We need to talk about talk. And we need to talk about how children talk. How do we do this? This chapter will introduce you to the language you need. But why do we need to do this? Let us start by considering some good reasons.

One important consideration is that you may wish to discuss a child's language development with a colleague, or indeed the person with responsibility for special or additional educational needs. Maybe you simply feel some vague concern about a particular child, or are unsure about how to assess a child's language development. This may be because this is a bilingual child, who is either fully bilingual or at the early stages of learning English and thus becoming bilingual – often referred as English as an additional language (EAL) in the UK – or because you suspect some kind of difficulty in linguistic development. Equally, you may wish to assert or confirm that a child is developing within a generally accepted developmental window. You may wish to develop the knowledge and understanding needed to become a school leader in the area of language and literacy development. You may need to explain something to teaching assistants or offer some professional development to colleagues. You may simply want to be able prepare a report on a child's language development for referral to an outside agency such as the speech and language therapy service – or indeed to convey information in clear terms to parents and caregivers. This chapter will help you to do this. And later in the school curriculum you may indeed need to teach some terms to the children themselves. First of all, however, let us look at what you, the professional, need to know. The rest of this chapter will consider under each heading what we might need to know and name and then in the next chapter we will consider what sort of development we might expect in these areas of language. Accordingly, we will look in turn at the following: vocabulary, grammar (syntax and morphology), phonology (the sound system) and pragmatics (the social rules that govern language use). We will then also consider what children use language *for* – as there is so much more to think about than the 'nuts and bolts' of grammar, vocabulary and so on. In the next chapter, we will develop this further by looking at what we can expect in a typically developing child, as, of course, phonological, grammatical, lexical, semantic and pragmatic development are all happening at once. Our focus will initially be on a monolingual child learning English, but, as we shall see in Chapters 5 and 6, monolingualism is far from the norm around the world, and we will look there at the complexity and richness of language development in a bi- or plurilingual child. For now, we will consider what happens with just one language, illustrated with reference to English.

One key thing we need to keep in mind is the distinction between receptive and productive language – in other words, what children understand and what they can produce. Although we are focusing upon children's talk, of course this cannot happen without them understanding others. From the minute they are born, and indeed before, babies are surrounded by sound, so let us start with some concepts that are important to understand in their own right before we consider how children actually develop language.

PHONOLOGICAL DEVELOPMENT

Phonological development is essentially the development of the sound system. As adult users of a language, most of us take for granted that we are able to perceive and reproduce the numerous sounds of the language(s) we speak. This is, however, another feat for the baby to perform – not only to perceive and process incoming sounds, but also to learn the sophisticated tricks of waggling the tongue around and moving the mouth into different shapes to modify the airstream from the lungs. This is a truly amazing human ability. So what do we mean by phonology? As Yule (1985: 44–5) says, it is essentially a description of the systems and patterns of speech sounds in a language. He points out that it is basically a theory of what speakers of a language unconsciously know about the sound patterns of their language, and that, therefore, phonology is concerned with the mental or abstract aspects of the sounds rather than their physical articulation. But what are these sounds?

PHONEMES

Phonemes are the smallest meaningful units of sound in a language, signalling a contrast in meaning. For example, /p/ contrasts with /b/ to signal the difference between 'pat' and 'bat'. Indeed, Yule (1985: 45) states that an essential property of a phoneme is that it functions contrastively. It is, nevertheless, an abstract concept. This is because the way a sound comes out varies according to the surrounding sounds. So take the words 'pat', 'too' and 'eighth' – in fact, each rendering of the **phoneme** /t/ is slightly different. It's a **phone**, and an **allophone** of the phoneme /t/. To transcribe it *phonetically* (as a speech therapist might need to), rather than *phonemically*, we use square brackets [ ]. The number of phonemes varies according to language, as is clearly illustrated by the International Phonetic Alphabet (IPA, 1949; 1999), a language-neutral set of symbols that represent all the sounds of the world's languages. In English we have 44 phonemes (although this may vary slightly according to region, because of variation in accents). There are 24 **consonant** phonemes and twenty **vowel** phonemes. The latter often comes as a surprise to people as we tend to think in terms of the written language rather than the sounds of the language, so many of us think of English as having five vowels (a, e, i, o, u). So, of course, another surprise (or maybe not!) is that we only have 26 letters (or graphemes), thus making the relationship between sounds (phonemes) and letters (graphemes) rather complex. To return to the issues of sound production, the basic principle of producing sounds is that there is a body of moving air from the lungs which is obstructed or modified in some way. Vowels are formed by shaping the mouth/tongue around the air coming up from the lungs, without the tongue touching the roof or sides of the mouth, whereas consonants are formed by obstructing the air in some way. If you have never tried this before, read a few sentences out loud and concentrate hard on what is actually happening in your mouth. This should highlight the fast and sophisticated 'footwork' your mouth and tongue are undertaking!

CONSONANTS

Consonants are normally given a three-part description: manner (of obstruction), place (in the mouth) and voice (whether they are voiced or not). Manner and place are perhaps self-explanatory but what do voiced and voiceless mean? We need to understand that air comes from the lungs, via the trachea (wind pipe), to the larynx (voice box). Once there, it must pass through the glottis (the space between the vocal chords). If the glottis is open, and the vocal chords are therefore apart, the air escapes unimpeded. This produces voiceless sounds. If the vocal chords are close together, the air will force them apart, making them vibrate. This produces voiced sounds, so, for example, /s/ is voiceless and /z/ is voiced. How can we test this? Try the following:

(a) hold larynx (voice box) and say /s/ and /z/ alternately;
(b) put fingers in ears and do the same;
(c) try humming /s/ and /z/.

Try this on pairs of voiced and voiceless consonants and see if you can tell the difference. We should note that it is a convention to write the voiceless sound on the left and the voiced on the right on phonemic alphabet charts, where the voiced and voiceless are presented in pairs.

However, let us return to the three-part description of consonants. Here we use the symbols from the IPA, but you will see that some are identical to the letters of the Roman alphabet, the script, or writing system, used by English.

MANNER

STOP/PLOSIVE
The articulators come together and cut off the flow of air momentarily, then separate abruptly. The plosives are: p b   t d   k g

FRICATIVE
The articulators are brought close together, creating a narrow channel through which air squeezes on its way out, producing turbulence. These are:

f v   s z   θ ð   ʃ ʒ   h

Some of these symbols may be unfamiliar. The symbols θ and ð represent respectively the 'th' sound in 'thin' and 'the', two different phonemes. You may not have realised that the spelling <th> actually represents two different phonemes. The symbols ʃ and ʒ represent respectively the 'sh' sound in 'sheep' and the 'je' sound in 'measure'. We tend to only have this word medially, but in French it occurs frequently in word-initial position, as in 'je' meaning 'I' and 'jambon' meaning 'ham'!

AFFRICATES
The articulators come together and cut off the flow of air, but separate gradually. There are two of these:

tʃ   dʒ

Again, you may ponder over these, but if you look carefully you will see that they each combine a plosive and a fricative. The symbol t ʃ represents the 'ch' sound in 'chicken' and the symbol dʒ represents the 'j' sound in 'jam'. So, this means that 'chicken' actually starts with /t/, and 'jam' with /d/. This sometimes shows up in young children's early attempts at spelling (Read, 1975)!

NASAL

Air escapes through the nose – the velum (soft palate) is lowered to allow access to the nasal tract. When you have a cold, the air cannot escape through the nose so you end up producing a plosive instead, as in, for example, the word 'tummy' coming out as something like 'tubby' ! The nasal consonants are:

m   n   ŋ

The symbol ŋ represents the 'ng' in 'hang'.

LATERAL

The air is obstructed but the sides of the tongue are left low, so that air escapes over one or both sides. The only one in English is: l

APPROXIMANT

The articulators are brought near each other, but a large enough gap is left for air to escape without turbulence. These are: w   r   j The symbol /j/ represents the 'y' sounds in eg, yacht or young

PLACE

You will need to refer to the diagram of the organs of speech (Figure 2.1). This shows, among other things, the key places in the mouth involved in the production of the phonemes of English. The following list sets out these places in the mouth and their related labels: lips – labial; teeth – dental; alveolar ridge – alveolar; palate – palatal; velum – velar; glottis – glottal.

VOICE

We saw above how consonants are either voiced or voiceless. The consonants /s/ and /z/ both share place and manner: place is alveolar and manner is fricative. They are both therefore alveolar fricatives. However, they are two separate phonemes in English; there is meaningful distinction between these two sounds. What then distinguishes them from each other? As we saw above, it is voice.

Describing consonants, then, requires this three-part description, so that, for example, we can describe /f/ as a voiceless, bilabial fricative.

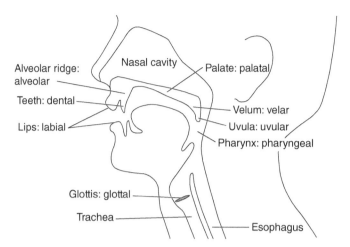

Figure 2.1

VOWELS

As we noted above, English has 20 vowel phonemes. Unlike consonants, vowels are all voiced and there are no obstructions from the articulators. Vowels are generally described in terms of how high and how far back in mouth they are and also how closed the lips are and the symbols are set out in a diagram accordingly (see Appendix II). However, there are two kinds of vowel in English: monopthongs and dipthongs. **Monopthongs** are pure vowels and there are twelve of them, seven short and five long. The long vowels are marked with: so that, for example, we would have a short vowel in a word such as 'bin', transcribed as /ɪ/ and a long one such as the vowel in 'been' transcribed as /iː/. What are the **diphthongs**? If you look at the chart in Appendix II that shows how the symbols represent the orthography of English you'll see them set out separately on the right hand side of the chart in bold. The following words in the chart have dipthongs in them: *here, day, tour, boy, go, pear, my* and *now*. There are eight of them and they essentially consist of two vowels, where one glides into the other. So, if you look closely at the symbols, you'll see that each is a combination of two of the short vowels. For example, the vowel diphthong you hear in a word such as 'day' is /e/ and /i/ combined as /ei/. Not all languages have dipthongs so they can be tricky for speakers of other languages to learn.

Finally, the importance of learning phonemic discrimination is illustrated by the notion of **minimal pairs**. Many pairs of words are distinguished from each other by only one phoneme. So, for example, the words 'zip' and 'sip' have only one phonemic difference, that between /z/ and /s/.

STRESS AND INTONATION

In this section on the development of the sound system, we now need to consider **stress and intonation**. First, a word about stress: the world's languages are generally considered to be either stress-timed or syllable-timed (Clark and Yallop, 1990: 288). In a stress-timed language, such as English, the stress falls at regular intervals, regardless of the number of syllables. In a syllable-timed language, such as French, all the syllables receive a roughly equal amount of stress. This clearly has implications for the listener. If you <u>read</u> this <u>sen</u>tence al<u>oud</u> you will <u>hear</u> the <u>stress</u> <u>fall</u>ing at <u>reg</u>ular <u>in</u>tervals. Now try reading it again and giving each syllable the same amount of stress – it will sound quite different. A further issue is that in English we can add additional stress in places to subtly alter the meaning – try saying aloud 'I didn't know your mother was a professor' several times, placing heavy stress on each word in turn. A further little feature of English (beloved of crossword setters) is the way in which word stress alters a word from a noun to a verb – words such as 'present', 'record' and 'permit' are nouns when you stress the first syllable and verbs when you stress the second syllable – try it!

Finally, there is intonation – the rising and falling of tones. Intonation tells the listener if they are being asked something or told something, to offer an obvious example. It can also convey an expectation on the speaker's part. Compare a request such as 'you're going to make the dinner, aren't you?' with a rising or falling intonation on 'aren't you?' One signals that this is not really a question but an instruction and the other that it *is* a question.

Of course, as we have already seen, the sound system conveys meaning in three ways, through phonemes, stress and intonation. However, the meaning comes not just from the sound system, but from words and grammar. Let us look next at *words*, the lexicon.

LEXICAL DEVELOPMENT

Vocabulary is known by linguists as the lexicon, basically consisting of all the words that a speaker of a language knows. The lexicon can also refer to all the words in a language. Leaving aside for the moment the issue of receptive and productive vocabulary (that is, what we can recognise versus what we can ourselves produce), guidance tends to focus on the *number* of words that we can reasonably expect children (or adults) to know. However, as we shall see, there is much more to lexical development than this.

Perhaps the first interesting distinction to make in this area is between what linguists call 'open' and 'closed' classes of words. So what belongs in each class of words? The 'open' class consists of nouns, verbs, adjectives and adverbs, whereas the 'closed' class includes prepositions, determiners, pronouns and conjunctions, thus eight major word classes in total. 'Open' class words constantly admit new members – for instance, when new things are invented, names for them can and must be invented too. In recent years, for example, words such as 'email', 'internet', 'hashtag' and 'meme' have joined our lexicon, as did 'radio' and 'television' before them. Old words are also used in new ways, such as 'ghosting' and 'trolling', reflecting the social developments of our times. Yet no new articles have arrived to add to or usurp 'a' 'an' and 'the', and prepositions such as 'on' 'to' and 'at' are equally safe and unthreatened by cheeky new upstarts. Thus, the open class is infinite and ever expanding, whereas the closed class is just that – a finite and closed set.

Let us start with a grammatical description of these different **kinds of words**. Words are generally agreed to belong to a word class or a grammatical category. As we say above, there are eight of these but we will start with the ones that belong to the open class of words. First up: **nouns**! A fairly traditional way of talking about nouns is to see them as referring to persons or things, but a more accurate and grammatical way of identifying them in English is to apply a 'noun test'– can you use the articles 'the' or 'a/an' with the word? This will work with common nouns such as 'apple' or 'shoe', but there are also what are known as proper nouns, which reference a specific person, place, thing, animal or idea and in English are marked with a capital letter, e.g. London or Maria. Another reason a grammatical test is useful is because some words can be both: for example, in the utterance 'I dance' 'dance' is a verb but in the utterance 'I enjoyed the dance', 'dance' is a noun. A further issue regarding nouns to bear in mind is that nouns can be **countable** or **non-countable** (the latter sometimes called 'mass'), so words like 'girl' and 'bird' are countable whereas words like 'milk' and 'rain' are not: in other words, they generally cannot have a plural –s, nor can they have 'a' or 'an' in front of them. However, there are numerous examples of words that can be both countable and non-countable. In a café, for example, one might request 'two milks', which might be served in 'glasses' (countable) made of 'glass' (uncountable).

Verbs are up next: again, there used to be a tradition of calling these 'doing words'. This is, however, unhelpful because other kinds of words may imply some sort of action (e.g. in our example above, with the word 'dance', the noun implies as much action or 'doing' as the verb); equally, there are verbs that do not really imply action, such as 'seem', 'be' or 'like'. Is there a test for a verb? The best way to do this is to see if the word can be made into present tense, by adding a third person –s, such as (he) walk–s and/or by adding past tense –ed, (he) walk–ed. There are of course numerous irregular verbs that do not follow this pattern, such as 'eat' becoming 'ate' in the past tense. There are also **auxiliary** verbs, such as 'to have' (I have eaten) and 'to be' (I am eating) as well as **modal** verbs that can alter the meaning of other verbs. They can express meanings such as certainty, possibility or obligation. The main modal verbs are *will, would, can, could, may, might, shall, should, must* and *ought (to)*. And then these two can combine to form **modal auxiliary** verbs in such utterances as 'I could have', or 'we should have' to talk about hypothetical experiences. Without these we cannot speculate about what might or could happen in the future or what could have been the case in the past. And of course when these constructions are used with negatives and/or questions, they are very complex, as in, for example: 'could we not have ordered those books online?'

And now to **adjectives** and **adverbs**: both of these have modifying roles, adjectives to modify nouns and adverbs to modify verbs or adjectives. In the case of **adjectives**, again the traditional way of describing adjectives is to call them 'describing words', but this is unhelpful for similar reasons to verbs and nouns. Something apparently obvious like describing the colour of something can be done with a verb, adverb or noun ('the sea was such a lovely blue!') as well as an adjective. If an adjective, this can be before a noun, modifying the noun to give it a more specific meaning as in 'the blue sea' or after the verb *be*, as its complement, as in 'the sea was blue'. What about **adverbs**? Their role is to modify verbs or adjectives, as in 'he was laughing loudly' (verb modified) or 'the job was really awful' (adjective modified by the adverb 'really').

We have so far looked at four of the major word classes in English, but there are the four others mentioned above: **prepositions**, **determiners**, **pronouns** and **conjunctions**. These, however, belong in the closed class category as they are finite in number. Prepositions include words such as *to, on, in, for, at* and often describe locations or directions, but can denote other things, such as time. **Determiners** include articles (*the, a* or *an*), demonstratives (e.g. *this, those*); possessives (e.g. *my, your*); quantifiers (e.g. *some, every*). A determiner goes before any modifiers such as adjectives or other nouns, as in, for example, 'my green bag'. **Pronouns** are used much like nouns, so that we do not always have to repeat the noun – e.g. in an utterance like 'Jenny loves ice-cream', we can also say 'she likes it'. I, you, he, she, it, we, they, me, him, her, us and them are all personal pronouns. Possessive pronouns are words like 'mine' as in, 'this is my bag' can be also expressed as 'this is mine'. **Conjunctions** link two words, phrases or clauses together. There are two main types of conjunctions, the first of which is coordinating conjunctions (e.g. *and*) which link two words or phrases together as an equal pair, and the second is subordinating conjunctions (e.g. *when*) which introduce a subordinate clause. We will look at these concepts in a little more detail when we consider grammar.

Before we do, however, a further consideration is what it is that words refer to. In other words, what do the words mean? Many words have multiple meanings – consider, for example, the word 'bat' in English. Is this a winged night creature or something you play table tennis or cricket with? Or is it something you actually *do*, for example in cricket but not in table tennis? A further point is that one word may have both physical/literal and metaphorical properties. The word 'sweet' can mean literally tasting sweet or it can mean a personal trait in a person or perhaps refer to a kind gesture. Equally, 'hard' can be a hard surface or something difficult. These are sometimes known as double-function words (Nippold, 2016: 52).

What are the relationships that words have with each other? These may be grammatical relationships – for instance, 'tolerant', 'tolerance' and 'tolerate' are clearly related to each other grammatically as well as semantically. But there may also be a relationship of synonymy or antonymy – that is, words may have the same or similar meaning as other words (synonyms), or they may be opposites (antonyms). Children themselves will draw their own conclusions at times – one small child we knew thought that the opposite of 'real' was 'pretend' while another thought that the opposite of 'real' was 'plastic'! Another issue is that of superordinates. These are words that refer to a category, such as 'bird', rather than the members of such a group like 'robin', 'sparrow' and so on.

And what does the closed class mean for children? We might be tempted to think that in the case of closed class words, this represents a relatively simple task. However, this is far from the case – they really do have to be learned in context as they mean so little in isolation. Consider, for example, a preposition such as 'on'. This may be simple at first glance – 'on the table' is quite clearly different and distinct from 'under the table'. This is, of course, only one interpretation of the word 'on' – a literal and quite concrete (even visible) one which needs to be compared to other uses such as 'on the television', 'on the wall', 'on time' and 'on that point ...' – never mind its use in what are called phrasal verbs – 'put on', 'take on' and so on. Readers with experience of other languages will spot straightaway that these do not translate directly! Thus it should quickly become apparent that the language that young children are exposed to (the input) and the opportunities they have to use it appropriately are of crucial importance. Small wonder, then, given that they have to process the stream of speech without recourse to the knowledge of word boundaries that literacy knowledge confers upon language users, that our three-year-old friend asked for his 'coaton', having so often heard 'put your coat on'!

So, young children have quite a task in learning how to understand and use all these words. As we will see in more detail in Chapter 3, their first task is to extract words from the input and assign them some meaning. As noted above, the stream of speech – even if somewhat modified for the young child – offers something of a challenge to a non-literate infant. It is generally thought that children probably understand their first 50 words before they produce them. By the age of eighteen months, most children have a vocabulary of 50 words in production, and between two and three times more in comprehension (Hulit and Howard, 2006). That young children do this is an impressive achievement. This is all the more so when we consider that all these words have to be ordered into a grammar.

GRAMMAR

Grammar essentially consists of syntax and morphology. We will take morphology first, as this follows on quite naturally from looking at words. **Morphology** is the study of the internal structure of words – the smallest meaning-bearing units of language are termed 'morphemes'. Simple words, on the one hand, do not have an internal structure as they only consist of one morpheme (e.g. dance, laugh, work). These are also called 'free' morphemes as they stand alone with a specific meaning. Words like these cannot be split into smaller meaningful units. Complex words, on the other hand, do have an internal structure and consist of two or more morphemes. This can be two 'free' morphemes as in 'blackberry' (both 'black' and 'berry' can stand alone) or a free and a bound morpheme e.g. walker: the bound morpheme –er is added to the root word to form a noun. Similarly, we could add –ness to some words, producing, say, calmness. The morphemes –er and –ness cannot stand alone. These additions are affixes. Those that come after are *suffixes*, as in the examples just given, whereas those that come before are *prefixes* such as un- and dis-.

DERIVATIONAL AFFIXES

An affix can be either derivational or inflectional. Derivational affixes serve to alter the meaning of a word by building on a base. In the examples of words with prefixes and suffixes above, the addition of the prefix un– to healthy alters the meaning of healthy. The resulting word means 'not healthy'. The addition of the suffix –er to garden changes the meaning of garden, which is a place where plants, flowers, etc. grow, to a word that refers to 'a person who tends a garden'. It should be noted that *all* prefixes in English are derivational. However, suffixes may be either derivational or inflectional.

INFLECTIONAL AFFIXES

There are a large number of derivational affixes in English. In contrast, there are only eight inflectional affixes in English, and these are all **suffixes**. English has the following inflectional suffixes, which serve a variety of grammatical functions when added to specific types of words. These grammatical functions are shown to the right of each suffix, along with an example.

　　–s　　noun plural, e.g. dog*s*

　　–'s　　noun possessive, e.g. dog*'s*

–s   verb present tense third person singular, e.g. he jump*s*

–ing   verb present participle, e.g. I am jump*ing*

–ed   verb simple past tense, e.g. she jump*ed*

–en   verb past participle, e.g. we have eat*en*

–er   adjective comparative, e.g. this one is small*er*

–est   adjective superlative, e.g. this one is the small*est*

SYNTAX

So clearly there is a relationship between words and grammar, but this is not just a question of how words change; it is also about syntax, the ways in which words are ordered. Syntax is essentially sentence structure. First, there are different types of sentence. Perera (1984: 19), following Crystal *et al.* 1976, suggests that there is an important distinction between major and minor utterances. Minor utterances are those that might also be considered 'formulaic', such as 'good afternoon' or 'thank you very much', principally used in social situations. Major utterances, on the other hand, are highly productive and creative, and importantly can be **full** or **elliptical**. Ellipsis is simply the process of omission and this typically happens in answers to questions, for example:

Q: What time is dinner?
A: About eight.

Here, what is omitted is 'dinner is', as in the full sentence 'dinner is about eight'. This means, of course, that people for much of the time do not actually talk in full sentences (unless they are making some formal presentation). It also means that if we want to establish whether a child can produce a statement, we need to use a prompt such as 'tell me about …'. This is why we talk about children's *utterances* rather than sentences.

So what exactly is a sentence? According to Perera (1984: 20–1), there are four sentence functions that have a regular correlation with grammatical form: statements, questions, commands and exclamations, of which the statement is the basic type from which the others are derived. Statements can be of three sorts – simple, compound and complex. Before we continue, however, we need to understand the concepts of 'subject' and 'object'. The **subject** is the person or thing doing something, and the **object** is having something done to it. In a sentence such as 'I eat carrots', I is the subject and carrots is the object of the sentence. A simple sentence can be just subject and verb (SV) – e.g. He laughed, or SVO (subject, verb, object). This is what we call a main clause. What we put in subject position or object position are not simply nouns, but more accurately described as **noun phrases**. This means that we can add determiners, adjectives and so on to the noun. Consider the following sentences:

Rabbits eat carrots

    S   V   O

The big fat fluffy white rabbits eat long juicy organic carrots.

          S   V   O

The big fat fluffy white rabbits have been eating long juicy organic carrots.

          S   V   O

So 'rabbits' is a noun phrase and 'the big fat fluffy white rabbits' is a noun phrase and 'long juicy organic carrots' is also a noun phrase. In the same way, it is more accurate to refer to the verb as a **verb phrase**, so both 'eat' and 'have been eating' are verb phrases.

The important thing to note here is that in all three sentences above, the structure is the same. They are *all* **simple sentences**. Adverbs or adverbial phrases can also be added. For example, we could perhaps add the adverbial phrase 'in the garden'.

So what is a **compound sentence**? This is where two simple sentences are joined by conjunctions *or, and* or *but*, as in, for example, I like chips but I hate ketchup. In this example, 'I like chips' and 'I hate ketchup' could stand alone as simple sentences/main clauses.

This is different from complex sentences. A complex sentence consists of a **main clause** and a **subordinate clause**. The subordinate clause is introduced by a subordinating conjunction, such as 'when' or 'because', as in, for example, 'the boy was eating, because he was hungry'. Note that 'the boy was eating' is a main clause and 'because he was hungry' is the subordinate clause. Unlike the main clause this cannot stand alone – unless of course it is an ellipted utterance in response to a question and therefore more of a feature of spoken than written language. Subordinate clauses can be finite or non-finite. **Finite verb** forms show tense, person and number (I go, she goes, we went, etc.). Finite simply means that the verb is conjugated, that is, attached to a particular person, whereas **non-finite verb** forms do not. So compare:

a) *After Charlie had eaten supper, he watched television.*
b) *Having eaten supper, Charlie watched television.*

In (a) we know immediately that it was Charlie eating supper, whereas in (b), until we get to the main clause (*Charlie watched television*), it could be anyone.

A final note here is that I have mentioned several times the differences between spoken and written language. Very young children are, of course, exposed to spoken language, but, as we shall see in Chapter 4, they later encounter the written form of the language, which introduces them to differences in these two modes of communication.

PRAGMATICS

The last section on pragmatics takes us in a slightly different direction, one of language in *use*. The understanding that language is so much more than a set of rules has a long history. The philosopher Ludwig Wittgenstein (1953) stressed the importance of how language is used to accomplish objectives. The work of Austin (1962), with a book entitled *How to Do Things with Words*, and Searle's (1969) book *Speech Acts*, were highly instrumental in establishing the field of speech act theory, leading us to pay more attention to how language actually achieves things.

So, working with young children, just as important as being able to describe their development in terms of grammar, lexicon and so on is the ability to describe what it is they are *doing* with all these words. Indeed, where there may be some doubt or concern about their grammatical or lexical development, it can be crucial to establish the meanings they are trying to convey as this will give some indication regarding their cognitive and/or social development. This is vital if your concern is that a child may have some kind of learning difficulty. Equally, a child may be very well developed in linguistic terms, but not conveying a full range of meanings or communicating in a socially appropriate way. So how do we use language? First of all, let us remind ourselves that when we describe language in a linguistic way – that is, the form of language – there is a generally agreed set of categories, as set out above. However, when we come to the **functions** of language, there is not really a simple parallel. What are the functions of language? We use language to report, to request, to complain, to impress, to explain and to describe, to give some examples. But there is more to this than choosing the grammatically and lexically correct items. Communicative competence refers to the appropriate use of language in social contexts, including when to speak and when not to speak (Hymes, 1972). This requires a number of things. First, as humans interacting with each other, we need 'theory of mind' – we need to be able to gauge what knowledge is shared between ourselves and those we are talking to. We also need to build up an understanding of how different social contexts require different language for the same function. The social context will dictate whether 'please close the door' or 'were you born in a barn?' is more appropriate and, additionally, there is the importance of understanding implied requests such as 'it's really cold in here'. The ability then to select the appropriate register for the social context, including the audience, is critical in becoming communicatively competent. Equally, within any cultural context, there are *topics* deemed suitable or otherwise for public discussion.

A final consideration is what we call **paralanguage**, the study of which is 'paralinguistics', a term coined by Trager (1958). Paralinguistic features include acoustic cues such as loudness, rate and pitch which help to convey attitudes and emotions, while other things such as sighing, gasping and throat clearing can also convey a speaker's views. Gestures are also very important, and have been extensively studied in children's development (see, for example, de Bot and Gullberg, 2010). Gestures can function in various ways: they may be imperative, trying to order the caregiver to do something, or declarative, trying to point something of interest out to the adult (Cochet and Vauclair, 2012). There are also what are known as representational gestures, which can be iconic, as they have a visually similar relationship to the thing they portray, such as waving your hand while describing hitting something. And, of course, there are also culturally contextualised gestures, such as nodding to indicate that you are agreeing or accepting something proposed by your interlocutor. In each culture, there is a commonly understood repertoire of gestures, which need to be learned in the same way as vocabulary, and which vary significantly from culture to culture.

CHAPTER SUMMARY

In this chapter, we have reviewed some key concepts in the study of language. These should be helpful to you in understanding the following chapters and in describing children's language should you need to. However, what makes the study and description of children's language challenging (albeit fascinating at the same time!) is that in the child many things are happening simultaneously. The development of the sound system, grammar, lexicon and pragmatic skills are closely intertwined. For that reason, the next two chapters will take us chronologically through what happens as the baby, then child, develops all these aspects of language.

REFERENCES

Austin, J.L. (1962) *How to Do Things with Words*. London: Oxford University Press.

Clark, J. and Yallop, C. (1990) *An Introduction to Phonetics and Phonology*. Oxford: Blackwell.

Cochet, H. and Vauclair, J. (2012) Pointing gesture in young children: hand preference and language development. In J.-M. Colletta and M. Guidetti (eds), *Gesture and Multimodal Development*. Amsterdam: John Benjamins.

de Bot, K. and Gullberg, M. (2010) *Gestures in Language Development*. Amsterdam: John Benjamins.

Hulit, L.M. and Howard, M.R. (2006) *Born to Talk: An Introduction to Speech and Language Development*. 4th edn. London: Pearson.

Hymes, D.H. (1972) On communicative competence. In J.B. Pride and J. Holmes (eds), *Sociolinguistics: Selected Readings*. Harmondsworth: Penguin.

International Phonetic Association (IPA) (1949) *The Principles of the International Phonetic Association*. London: International Phonetic Association.

International Phonetic Association (IPA) (1999) *Handbook of the International Phonetic Association: A Guide to the Use of the International Phonetic Alphabet*. Cambridge: Cambridge University Press.

Nippold, M.A. (2016) *Later Language Development: School-Age Children, Adolescents, and Young Adults*. 4th edn. Austin, TX: Pro-Ed. Inc.

Perera, K. (1984) *Children's Writing and Reading*. Oxford: Blackwell.

Read, C. (1975) Lesson to be learned from the per-school orthographer. In E.H. Lenneberg and E. Lenneberg (eds), *Foundations of Language Development*, vol. 2, 329–45.

Searle, J. (1969) *Speech Acts*. Cambridge: Cambridge University Press.

Trager, G.L. (1958) Paralanguage: a first approximation. *Studies in Linguistics*, 13, 1–12.

Wittgenstein, L. (1953) *Philosophical Investigations*. Oxford: Blackwell.

Yule, G. (1985) *The Study of Language*. Cambridge: Cambridge University Press.

PART II

MONOLINGUAL LANGUAGE DEVELOPMENT

3

EARLY LANGUAGE DEVELOPMENT: 0-5

INTRODUCTION

This chapter will set out the key developmental milestones that occur from birth to approximately age five. We will be looking at language development from a variety of perspectives at each stage that we study, including phonology, grammar, semantics/lexicon and pragmatics, concepts we introduced in Chapter 2. In taking the child's development stage by stage, it doesn't necessarily follow that each of these aspects will receive exactly the same amount of attention. For example, in looking at the first year, there is considerably less to say about grammar than, say, phonology. Indeed, the two aspects that will predominate in this first section will be phonology – the child's early acquisition of phonology, and pragmatics – how the child acquires the social rules of language, such as conversation.

BIRTH TO FIRST WORDS

To start with, we are going to concentrate on the first period of acquisition, from birth up to the point where first words appear. As we will see, it is not necessarily easy to define exactly when this point is. Moreover, there is a certain amount of individual variation such that different children may arrive at this point at different times. Very roughly, this can be from around ten months of age up until about fourteen months, so we are looking at the first year of life. We will look first at the child's acquisition of the phonological system, both in terms of the perception of phonology and of its production. After that, we will look at how adult–child interaction provides the context in which language is acquired.

THE ACQUISITION OF PHONOLOGY: PERCEPTION AND PRODUCTION

In order to fully appreciate the complexity of the acquisition process, you will need to have a grasp of the following: the notion of phonemes; how the vowel and consonant phonemes of English are produced; and the principle of phonemic discrimination (see Chapter 2). First of all, in terms of perception, what do babies have to do? One early task is to distinguish human sounds from non-human sounds. From the moment they are born, babies are surrounded by noise: traffic, dogs barking, kettles boiling, music, everyday kitchen sounds, water running … the list is endless. Not only do they need to work out which sounds are human, they also need to detect differences between human sounds, as not all of these are speech sounds. Humans laugh, burp, blow raspberries, cough and so on as well as talk. Babies have to acquire not just a sound system, but a *phonological* system. This means that they have to learn which phonemes they are exposed to (and in the case of bi- or plurilingual babies, this is more than one set) and, crucially, which phonemic contrasts are meaningful. The following anecdote may illustrate this. In English, the phonemes /p/ and /b/ create a meaningful distinction. They are both plosives, so the same manner of articulation, and they are both bilabial, so the same place of articulation. But they differ in terms of voice as /p/ is unvoiced and /b/ is voiced. This is a meaningful distinction in English but not in all the world's languages. Babies are born international so this must be learned. A young acquaintance of ours at the age of fifteen months, developing typically, was asked by a family friend to bring certain pieces from a wooden jigsaw featuring characters from a TV series called the *Magic Roundabout*. When asked to bring 'Paul', before we had a chance to say that she didn't know that one, she had gone to the living room and returned … with a ball! Out of context, she was not yet able to discriminate /b/ and /p/, although at some level, there was clearly an awareness of at least the similarity.

HOW AND WHEN DOES THIS PROCESS BEGIN?

It is well established that monolingual infants have sophisticated perceptual abilities from early on (Jusczck, 1997). Although the womb has what
Brookes and Kempe call a 'muffling' effect, babies can still detect rhythm
and intonation, thus allowing them 'considerable pre-natal experience'
(2012: 29). They are capable of recognising their mother's voice within the
first few days of life (DeCasper and Fifer, 1980), and of distinguishing
between the maternal language and another (unfamiliar) one at a few days
old (Mehler *et al.*, 1988). In the case of infants raised in a bilingual environment, Bosch and Sebastián-Gallés (2001) found that their Spanish-Catalan
subjects proved capable of detecting the difference between the two languages below five months of age, despite the languages having some
similarities in rhythm and intonation. Identifying the prosodic features of
language is one thing, however, but quite another is deciphering the phonemes of the language(s) the baby is exposed to. We saw in Chapter 2 that
the phoneme is an abstract concept, and that the different *allophones* are
acoustically slightly different from each other. As adults we cease to be
aware of these differences and come to assume that the phoneme /t/ in
'pat', 'too' and 'eighth' is the same in each word. In other words, we perceive them categorically – we class the different sounds as a category. This
is also key to understanding the relationship between phonemes and
graphemes in order to become literate. But how does the baby arrive at
these categories? As long ago as 1971, a seminal study by Eimas *et al.*,
using a high-amplitude sucking technique, demonstrated that one- and
four-month-old infants could in fact perceive the contrast between /p/ and
/b/. In other words, at an early age it appears that they are able to set up
these categories. Furthermore, babies are, of course, born international,
capable of discriminating contrasts from any of the world's natural languages (Kuhl, 1991). When you consider that these contain some 600
consonants and 200 vowels (Ladefoged, 2004), this is no mean feat.
Gradually, too, at about eight months, they start to show some sensitivity
to frequently occurring words or sound sequences. As Brooks and Kempe
point out (2012: 38), specific syllable combinations will occur often in
speech to children because the sequences of syllables comprise frequently
used words.

What, however, do babies produce in this early period? Clearly, the baby's
growing ability to produce sounds is a rather more observable (or audible!)
process. A lot of work goes on before the baby utters her or his first 'real'
word. Where does this process start? All those who have had any sustained
contact with very young babies are aware that their crying is by no means
always the same. Parents attempt to differentiate between cries of hunger,
pain, boredom and so on – with varying degrees of success. The first two
months or so are typically characterised by crying and vegetative sounds

like burping and sneezing, sometimes known as 'Stage 1' reflexive vocalisation (Vihman, 1996: 103). The thing that this kind of sound production has in common is that they are all 'basic biological noises' (Crystal, 1987). According to Vihman, cooing and laughter follow (age two to four months) and a third stage follows between four and seven months, which she describes as 'vocal play'. At around this time, a fairly prolonged period of what we call **babbling** begins, lasting until approximately fifteen months. Strictly speaking, we should break this period up, because 'real' babbling doesn't start until about six months. Prior to this there is a period of cooing and laughing that begins around two months, at times interspersed with vowel- or consonant-like sounds. Yells, squeals, raspberries and other sounds are also noticeable between three and six months, but gradually the baby babbles more and more vowel- and consonant-type sounds, and this continues despite the onset of first words, sometime between ten and fifteen months.

But why do babies babble? Basically, the infant is gaining control of her articulatory apparatus (which is also developing physiologically, of course). What kinds of sounds do they produce? At the beginning of the babbling period, glottal and labial sounds predominate. This is followed by the baby babbling approximants and laterals, with plosives and nasals appearing before the onset of first words. The vowels tend to be low rather than high, and the syllable structure is CV (consonant-vowel); they tend not to babble consonant clusters. Later babbling, around eight to nine months, is basically of two types: sound play, which is much as it sounds, and canonical babbling, also known as reduplicated babbling. It is produced using repeated syllables that consist of a consonant and a vowel, such as 'ba ba ba ba'. This is later followed by conversational babble, also referred to as modulated babble or expressive jargon. It is somehow 'social' in nature and as such tends to elicit responses from adults as if the child were really speaking. Gradually, babies approximate the sounds they produce to resemble increasingly the language they are hearing. Having started off international, they become increasingly attuned to their own language and from about six months of age an initial ability to identify phoneme contrasts from all of the world's languages declines (Saxton, 2017: 130). Are some phonemes acquired before others, however? The answer to this seems to be 'yes'. Generally speaking, in terms of consonants, bilabial and alveolar plosives such as /m/ and /t/ appear before velar plosives such as /k/ and fricatives such as /f/, with affricates such as / t ʃ/ (as in <chair>) somewhat later (see Cruttenden, 1979). By the end of the babbling period, however, babies have progressed from first vowels to a range of consonants (although by no means all), produce single syllables or sometimes two syllables together and have learned quite a lot about the rhythm and sound patterns of their language. Another reason for this early language development is also a conversational one.

THE CONTEXT OF LANGUAGE ACQUISITION: ADULT–CHILD INTERACTION

Looking at adults interacting with babies shows very clearly how the linguistic exchanges (such as they are!) are tightly integrated with other types of interaction that rely on other channels of communication. For example, researchers have noted the importance of **eye contact** – adults monitor closely the developing ability of the new-born infant to focus; later, play routines (peek-a-boo) help to direct and maintain the baby's gaze. Visual and tactile stimulation (smell too?) are both likely to be important in the language acquisition process – but, more generally, these channels allow the construction of an affectionate and loving bond between the caregiver/parent and the child. This is a point that is important when we consider how language is acquired, as the quality of this bond is important – such a huge emotional investment must play a part in the child's development. There are, of course, implications not just for parents but also for teachers and other caregivers.

It is generally agreed that language addressed to children has certain characteristics which can be categorised under the following headings:

1. prosodic features – stress and intonation;
2. lexical features – vocabulary with child in mind;
3. complexity features – simpler than speech addressed to adults;
4. redundancy features – for example, a lot of repetition;
5. content features – content that is child appropriate.

(Based on Ingram, 1989: 132)

It is worth noting not only the specifically linguistic characteristics of the language parents and other caregivers use, but also their expectations vis-à-vis the child; the latter is treated as if they can understand even when they patently cannot. Saxton (2017) calls this 'tutorials for toddlers'! Babies do, of course, respond: coos, babbles, gurgles and even burps are accepted from the parent as conversational offerings, although research suggests that there is a subtle altering of what is accepted by the parent as 'conversation' as the child develops, notably as babbling develops and again as first words are produced by the child. In this way, the basics of conversational turn-taking are established long before the baby can actually speak. Indeed, parents usually try very hard to persuade the baby to take her/his turn, and often reward any offering with a great deal of attention. However, having looked at the ways in which adults converse with babies, we need to consider the baby's role in all this. The baby is arguably much more than a passive participant in the conversation. The question we need to ask is this: is there communicative intent on the part of the baby? It can be hard to establish whether a baby is intending to communicate or is simply responding to stimulation and/or practising sounds in her/his repertoire. Although sounds can be linked with situations– for example, different kinds of crying – we could hardly say that the baby intended these different sounds in any conscious way. However, if we observe a child doing the following, it begins to look like communication:

1. making eye contact while gesturing or vocalising/making sounds;
2. gestures;
3. vocalisations with consistent sounds and intonation patterns;
4. waiting for response from partner;
5. persistence and even modification on part of child.

Next, we need to consider the function of these early communicative attempts. It may be to regulate the parent's behaviour, in order to obtain something, for example ('Get me that drink!'). It can be to maintain social interaction ('Keep talking to me – I like it!') or indeed to create joint attention ('Let's both stare at my mobile!'). Although babies can't actually say these things, they are laying the groundwork for when they do have actual words their disposal.

In summary, then, the interaction that takes place in the first nine to twelve months of the baby's life lays down the ground rules for linguistic exchanges within a particular culture, and establishes for the baby channels of communication and conversational strategies before the first real words appear. Over the course of this first period, the baby (while never really a passive participant) gradually learns to communicate with intent with the other people in her/his world.

ONE WORD AT A TIME

Although the study of language acquisition includes development at the phonological, grammatical, semantic and pragmatic levels, we focused in the first section on the development of phonology and of pragmatics, as these are the two areas most relevant to the first nine or twelve months of life. The latter is particularly important because it lays the foundations of communication and provides a context, both social and personal, within which children, in Halliday's (1975) terminology, learn how to mean. As Pan and Gleason (2001: 125) explain:

> Children understand the pragmatic intent of adults' utterances before they understand the words themselves. A toddler who begins to peel off his clothes on hearing his father say, 'It's time for your bath now,' may be responding to a variety of situational cues – it is a particular time of day, they are in a certain room, they are engaged in a familiar activity, or the parent may actually be pointing at the bathtub. Only very slowly do children come to understand and use words in adult fashion, to break them free of context and use them flexibly in a variety of situations.

In this section on first words, we are again going to consider the different levels of language development, bearing in mind that developments in phonology, grammar, semantics and pragmatics do, of course, occur at the same time. During the period of single-word utterances, however, grammar is less relevant than phonology, semantics and pragmatics. In the next section, when we look at word combinations, grammar will finally get a look in.

So when does this happen? **First 'word'**: this can be from 0:9 to 1:3, and is probably most common around the age of twelve months, about the time of the baby's first birthday. There may well be a discrepancy between **comprehension** and **production**, as children understand more words than they can produce. But once the first word has arrived it is followed by many more. This is gradual at first, possibly one per week (Saxton, 2017: 8), but usually by the age of about 18 months, children reach a further milestone, that of a 50-word vocabulary. This is generally seen as the point where things speed up, with one or two new words a day being acquired. A further acceleration takes place, sometimes known as the 'vocabulary spurt', between the ages of two and six, although Saxton cautions that individual differences are important (2017: 160). He nevertheless notes that by five years of age children have a vocabulary of several thousand words. It is not surprising that we then ask the question as to how many a day does this mean? Clark (1993), for example, suggests that ten words a day may be learned. The speed of this can seem bewildering to parents who may feel they can't keep up! But do these words have an adult-like pronunciation?

PHONOLOGY

How do children pronounce their first words? Look at the following examples and see if you can work out what is going on:

pudi tat (pussy cat)

guk (duck)

pider (spider)

paterkiller (caterpillar).

What processes/factors affect early pronunciation? Take the first example: 'pudi' for pussy – this is an example of **phonemic substitution**, where the fricative /s/ is replaced by the plosive /d/, both sounds made in the same place, both unvoiced, but the manner of articulation is different – it is easier to produce a plosive as you stop the air altogether whereas producing a fricative is trickier (try it!). This is why plosives tend to be acquired earlier than fricatives. Another example is 'tat' for cat – here a velar phoneme

/k/ (back of mouth) is replaced by alveolar (alveolar ridge) /t/. In this example, the manner is the same and both are unvoiced, but this time there is a different place of articulation.

Producing 'guk' for duck, however, is an example of **assimilation** where the /k/ sound at the end of the word duck influences the sound at the beginning and the infant gets her tongue to the back of the mouth too soon. The third example, 'pider' for spider is an example of **cluster reduction**, where one or more consonants in a cluster are omitted. Finally, 'paterkilar' for caterpillar, results from a process known as **metathesis** where all the sounds are there, but in the wrong order. These factors affecting early pronunciation are known as phonological processes and are entirely normal. A detailed understanding of these can assist speech and language therapists in deciding whether a child is developing in a typical way or not.

LEXICAL/SEMANTIC DEVELOPMENT

What *are* the first words and how can we tell when a child acquires their first word? We need to remember that 'acquire' can mean comprehension or production. With comprehension, infants will start to respond to familiar words by looking or reaching for something mentioned, although it is often difficult to establish whether the child is responding to the word being used or is relying on other non-linguistic information, as in the example about the bath above. Production is a more observable process. Let us think about the first words as used by the child. This is more difficult to define than one might expect – do we expect an adult-like pronunciation? If not, then what is acceptable? The child has to acquire the notion that words have meaning; once she or he consistently attaches the same utterance to the same thing, it is likely that she has reached the stage of recognising that words have referents, that there is a relationship between the word and the thing. It seems reasonable to 'count' as a word the utterance the child uses in that situation, even if the pronunciation is not the adult one. Indeed, the pronunciation itself may vary from one occasion to the next as the child tries to repeat the sound – that is, articulate it in the same way as before. Another thing to remember is that first 'words' may not necessarily name 'things', but may refer to a situation of some kind – for example, 'hot' might mean 'I mustn't touch that'. This is sometimes referred to the proto-word stage.

What **kinds of words** do children produce first? First words are likely to be ones that are easier to pronounce; this will typically mean, for example, in terms of place of articulation, labial before velar, and in terms of manner of articulation, plosives before fricatives. This is, of course, a simplification, and there will in any case be a certain amount of variation. Another factor may be the stage of cognitive development. There is some evidence that once the cognitive stage of object permanence (see Chapter 1) is reached, around the end of the first year, language that reflects this new awareness starts to be used – for example, 'there', 'allgone'. What kind of words do children actually use? Not surprisingly, young children talk about the objects that surround them. Nelson (1973) looked at the first ten words of eighteen children and found that the three categories referred to most often were animals, food and toys. The same children, at the stage where they had about 50 words (somewhere between the age of 1:3 and 1:9), were using words for food, body parts, clothing, animals, household items, vehicles and people. As we might also expect, children show a tendency to name things that they interact with, such as 'juice' (rather than 'wall' or 'corkscrew'). It is worth remembering, however, that there will be cultural influences on the actual words children use.

What do their first words **mean**? As pointed out above, first words don't necessarily have 'things' as referent; they may have whole situations. The child has the not inconsiderable task of 'unpacking' the combinations of words she/he hears all around. Word meanings, or the boundaries of word meanings, therefore take some time to be established. This may result in either underextension or overextension. Overextension is a feature of early language acquisition that is familiar to most people – the usual example is the child who addresses all men as 'daddy'! Children extend the meaning of single words as well as phrases. For example, one child called an old-fashioned gas fire with a grill a 'cot' and on seeing the wire mesh surrounding the tennis court said 'rabbit'. These over extensions can be based on one of a number of conceptual components: shape, movement, size, sound, texture and even taste (see Clark and Clark, 1977: 493–4). One well-known explanation of this phenomenon is Eve Clark's (1973) 'semantic feature hypothesis', which postulates that each word has a unique combination of semantic features, only some of which will be shared by other words, and that children begin to use words before they have a full knowledge of all their semantic features. A child might therefore assume that all things that share the features [male] and [human] and [tall] are referred to as 'daddy'. Underextension is less obvious (and not amusing in the same way as the overextension!), and in a sense continues well into later childhood and even adulthood (see Chapter 4). Even the more concrete referents may not be unambiguously established for some time so that words like 'ball' may be applied too specifically, to one particular ball.

PRAGMATIC DEVELOPMENT

Chapter 2 outlined the importance of pragmatics in language, noting that speakers of a language use it for a large range of purposes. As we saw, the form of language we select for any given purpose is constrained by the social context, and by the rules operating in that social context. Hence,

'Would you mind closing the door, please?' and 'It's freezing in here' are two different forms for conveying the same purpose (in this case a request to shut the door), but the choice of form is governed by social (unwritten) rules. Also, each of these two forms imply other unspoken messages. Similarly, 'That's hot' doesn't just convey factual information about the temperature of something, but also means 'You're not allowed to touch that'. Children have to learn how to comprehend and produce language in this way. Considering the way in which we translate our intentions into a particular form of language may give us insight into why children take some time to work out the meanings of words and phrases, and work out how to convey their own meanings linguistically. Children may be conveying a range of intentions with a single word: consider what 'juice!' might mean. It could mean, for example, 'you've got juice', 'give me the juice', 'I want juice', 'is this juice' and so on. There are, of course, problems with the interpretation of children's early words. The communicative intent that we noted as being a feature of the latter part of the first year (if not earlier) must be progressively encoded in language.

Language is used for myriad purposes, and children need to learn how to refuse, request, explain, persuade and so on, as appropriate to their audience. Among the various elements of this are the social formulae particular to the culture a child is growing up in. Obvious examples are words and phrases such as 'please', 'thank you' and 'excuse me', but others are less obvious. Children may come across as rude or gauche in certain situations, not least because working out the intentions and expectations of others can be tricky for young children. Young children often respond inappropriately (and sometimes amusingly) to adult prompts such as 'what do you say?', failing to recognise the cue for some formula. One anecdote about a three-year-old we know illustrates this: 'I want some juice' drew the response from his mother: 'what else do you say?', which in turn prompted the little boy to offer 'because I'm thirsty?'. This was without intending to be rude in any way – rather, a literal interpretation of what was expected. Gradually, however, by the time children reach school age, they have developed greater sensitivity to these cues, although much remains to be learned.

MULTI–WORD UTTERANCES

The period of using single words lasts until around eighteen to twenty months, although many children may not use **word combinations** until around about their second birthday. As we saw above, by this point many children will have 50 different words at their disposal. At this point children start to combine words, usually passing through a two-word stage lasting a number of months, before moving on to three-word combinations. Gradually, the number of words strung together increases, as the child's developing grammatical competence allows her to generate increasingly complex utterances. The move from one word to a combination of two words is generally regarded as a major developmental milestone. A child with, for example, 50 words at eighteen months, will vastly increase her linguistic output by using these in combination. Any new word acquired can then be used in combination with any of the words already in the child's repertoire – this gives the child the ability to generate language and as such is a vital step into the grammatical system. The next section will concentrate on the development of grammar, but we should remember that, at the same time, children will be developing their vocabulary, phonology and their pragmatic use of language. However, the acquisition of grammar is deserving of some considerable space in its own right. Indeed, Tager-Flusberg (1994: 185) describes the acquisition of grammar as 'one of the most remarkable and mysterious achievements of childhood'. Before we attempt to understand what an achievement this is, let us look first at what actually happens in terms of the child's language development.

How do we recognise the first two-word utterance? This may seem to be an unnecessary question. However, before two-word utterances appear, the child is likely to say two words in succession, but with separate intonation on each word and with a pause in between. Two single words in succession might be: Mummy. Chair. The child might later produce: Mummy chair. Research suggests that, over the period of single-word utterances, the single words are brought gradually closer together. This can mean that the first two-word utterance is actually quite difficult to determine. Just as children with one word seek to convey more complex meaning than just naming things, so they do when they have word combinations at their disposal. Thus, 'Daddy garden' could mean 'Daddy's in the garden'/ 'I want Daddy in the garden'/ 'Daddy was in the garden' and so on. Children at this stage will also produce two-word utterances where one of the words acts as a kind of 'pivot' (Braine, 1963). So, for example, the word 'more' is used with a range of other words, such as 'more milk', 'more book', 'more Mummy' – or, as a two-year-old we know said when looking at himself in the mirror, 'more me'! There will also be utterances that to the adult ear consist of two words – for example, all gone, bye bye, oh dear – but that the child has learned as a whole or as a routine. As we saw in Chapter 1, many children have unanalysed routines that can convey an air of sophistication! We mustn't forget how tricky it is to perceive word boundaries for young children. One little girl aged 3:7 said to her mother 'I bumped in' and, in response to her mother's puzzled look, added 'to daddy'.

As children move into their third year (for some children this may be as soon as their second birthday but others may be some months after this), their speech starts to include utterances that are different from the two-word ones in two ways: they are longer and they start to include inflections and different kinds of words. They use words from all grammatical categories: nouns, verbs, adjectives, adverbs and prepositions. However, we cannot overestimate the importance of the inflectional affixes (see Chapter 2), sometimes known as grammatical morphemes. This is a highly significant development because the grammatical morphemes allow us to give subtleties of meaning to what we say, they allow us, for example, to express concepts such as time and number. Acquisition of these is a gradual and lengthy process, which probably occurs within the period eighteen to 24 months, and takes until children are of school age, although often some irregularities are not fully mastered until well into the school years – for example, irregular past tense forms of some verbs. The most famous study of the acquisition of grammatical morphemes is the study by Brown (1973), who looked at fourteen grammatical morphemes of English. Brown found that there was an *order* of acquisition, so that, for example, the –ing that we add to verbs to give the present progressive (e.g. swimming) tended to be acquired first, followed later by the plural and possessive and even later by the past tense markers. Of course, in reality, language development is rather messier than a sequence suggests, but it is nevertheless important to be alert to what a typical developmental path looks like.

Understanding the typical sequence of acquisition is important to be able to pinpoint any possible problems, but we might also want to understand why things seem to follow an order. One explanation is that some things are just more salient because of their position in the sentence or maybe some inflections are stressed and others unstressed. For example, in the stream of speech it is quite hard to hear the past tense marker –ed. Another possible explanation is that parents or others looking after young children simply use some of the grammatical morphemes more frequently than others. After all, they are probably more likely to talk to young children about what is happening now than what happened yesterday, for example. This could explain the early appearance of –ing. Finally, some are more complex than others. The ending –ing is always the same, whereas the plural actually has three forms. If you compare glasses, cats and dogs, they all end in a different sound: glasses ends in –iz, cats in –s and dogs in –z!

LEARNING DIFFERENT TYPES OF SENTENCES: QUESTIONS, QUESTIONS, QUESTIONS!

So far, so easy! But as adult users of the language we probably don't even notice the complexity of the language we use. We don't simply make statements in language, we ask questions and young children must learn how to do this (understand and use) to interact with others.

There are basically two kinds of questions. First, we have what are called yes/no questions as potentially they could simply be answered with 'yes' or 'no', at least grammatically. Pragmatically this might be considered rude, of course, as in, 'would you like a cup of tea?' answered by 'no'. Of course, children have to learn these social pragmatic rules as well as the grammar. In order to form questions such as these, speakers can and do use intonation (e.g. 'tea?' 'you want tea?'), particularly in informal spoken language. However, English questions are what are called 'inverted' as they are the other way round to statements.

You are happy = statement

Are you happy? = question

However, to complicate matters, other verbs require the verb 'do' in order for questions to be formulated. For example:

you want   do you want?

she wants   does she want?

you wanted   did you want? etc.

To make this even trickier, English has a system of 'tag' questions.

You are coming, aren't you?

She isn't there, is she?

You like milk, don't you?

See if you can work out the rule! We will address this further in Chapter 4, however. For now, it is enough to point to the complexity of language that we possibly take for granted. It is hardly surprising that young children take some time to get all of this right and, although they use questions from a very early age, typically this will start by producing utterances with question intonation rather than the grammar. Then there is a second group of questions known as wh–questions because they start with what/where/who/why and how (obviously this does not start with wh– but it belongs to this group). Questions beginning with these words are open questions. There is a rough order in which children acquire these question words, with the what, who and where being acquired earlier than why and how. Even at the one-word or early two-word stage children will respond to questions with *what* and *who* and possibly *where*. They typically use *what's that?* with great frequency once they realise this generates an answer! Understanding and using questions with *why* and *how* comes later, usually about 2½ with *how* around three years of age or even later. The concepts embodied in cause and process are much more complex than those in *what* or *where*, and asking three- or even four-year-olds questions with 'how' is likely to prompt puzzlement or even a rather odd answer!

USING NEGATIVES: SAYING NO!

This is another important element to language development, as negatives are required to express non-existence, rejection or denial. Children do, of course, very quickly learn the words 'no' and 'not'! They often start with a single word and then progress simply to placing this before other words – 'no cot', 'no juice', 'not sleep'. However, they then have to develop the ability to use negation within sentences and questions. A next stage is when they place the negative word inside the sentence, as in, for example, 'I no see you'. Children then progress to using contracted forms like 'can't' and 'won't', in all likelihood regarding these as alternative forms of 'not', as at this stage they are not typically using auxiliary verbs like 'can' and 'will' in affirmative utterances (Peccei, 1994: 35). Gradually, with utterances having four or more words, auxiliary verbs appear in their own right and negative utterances become longer and more complex.

AUXILIARY VERBS: WHY THESE MATTER

Let's take the idea of predicting or relating to start with: in English if we want to talk about what has happened we have a simple past – I ate – or a perfect tense I have eaten. The latter needs an extra verb – have. Similarly, if we are to talk about the future we often need 'will'. Verbs such as these form part of a group of verbs called **auxiliary verbs**, so called because they 'help' to make up the verb phrase. Importantly, we also have **modal auxiliaries**, whose function is to express a mood or tense. These are shall, should, can, could, will, would, may, must and might. In the third and fourth year, children find their way into this complex system, but making many errors as they do so, which is hardly surprising, given the complexity of the rules. Without these auxiliary verbs, however, they cannot learn to speculate or hypothesise and their cognitive development and linguistic development are closely linked. Children therefore need opportunities to hear and use this much more complex language. Asking them to think and talk about what *might* or *could* happen is vital. And even more complex and thus more difficult is the speculation about, for example, what would have happened if, as this example from a child aged 4:9 illustrates: 'if we hadn't gone in Lynne's car and we hadn't gone in our car, how could we have got there … walked?' (Macrory, 2001). This example also illustrates the fact that children aren't tackling the business of learning to talk in the separate 'chunks' we have just outlined. In this example, the child is showing competence with questioning, negating and using auxiliaries. This does not mean, however, that there is a straightforward and neat progression, as the following examples from a diary study of my daughter illustrate. At age 2:3, 'what mummy doing?' is a pretty common occurrence, with the 'is' missing. At 3:2, nearly a year later, 'will you pick me up early 'cos I want to go to Katy's after nursery?' is quite impressive, yet a full year later at 4:3 'we must bring it to France, wouldn't we?' shows that the complexities of the language need time to disentangle, despite the correct utterance 'they won't fit me when I get big, will they?' aged 3:2! Similarly, at 2:3 the correct use of the negative is displayed in 'I don't want to fall off again', but a year later at 3:3, we have 'Katy didn't came to my party'. The tricky business of combining questions and negatives is reflected in 3:0 'why does it don't go in there?' Despite what may seem like rather uneven progress, however, the four-year-old can produce a variety of utterances that become more complex and lengthier, as in the following examples from the same child: at age 4:3 'when the dentist man had finished and was putting his things away, I sat on Daddy's knee' and, three months later, 'I'm not going to sleep unless I can go in your bed', 'if you hadn't brought my hat, I could have put my hood up' and 'I want to find a clean picture that hasn't been coloured in yet'. This does not, of course, mean that the utterances are error-free, hardly surprising when you consider that they are not only simultaneously learning to understand and produce sentences, questions and negatives, but also developing their vocabulary and their ability to communicate appropriately for their culture – no mean feat!

WHAT IS ALL THIS LANGUAGE FOR?

We have considered how children develop from single words to multi-word utterances, developing negatives and questions and using auxiliary verbs. Of course, they also learn imperatives and how to tell people what to do! But what do they *do* with this language? What do we all *do* with language? Unlike grammar there is no definitive list of functions of language, but we can all agree that this list would include the following: relate, suggest, describe, explain, hypothesise, justify, speculate, persuade, predict. In order to do this, as we have seen, during the third year children start to use more complex constructions. They start to join utterances with 'and', which allows them to produce longer and longer ones and they also start to use words like because, so, when and if – these allow them to convey more complex meaning relations. And language does not operate solely at sentence level. Sentences are increasingly joined together to create longer stretches of discourse that enable children to use language for an ever-increasing range of functions.

CHAPTER SUMMARY

In this chapter, I have given a brief overview of language development from birth to approximately age five. We have seen how language grows across all the domains: phonology, lexicon, grammar and pragmatics. We have seen too, how children come to use language for a variety of purposes. Equally, we saw that language development does not happen in a vacuum and, as we noted with the acquisition of questions, children are developing cognitively at the same time. Thus, they can only really use words like 'why' and 'because' when they understand the relationships between events or situations. Neither the correct linguistic forms nor the concepts behind them are mastered overnight, of course, and children are still working on all these aspects of development in the fourth and indeed the fifth year. The process of language acquisition is not complete even then, as we can see when we look at what is referred to as later language development, meaning, that is, the school years from five to eleven.

REFERENCES

Bosch, L. and Sebastián-Gallés, N. (2001) Early language differentiation in bilingual infants. In J. Cenoz and F. Genesee (eds), *Trends in Bilingual Acquisition Research*. Amsterdam: John Benjamins.

Braine, M.D.S. (1963) The ontogeny of English phrase structure: the first phase. *Language*, 39, 3–13.

Brookes, P.J. and Kempe, V. (2012) *Language Development*. Oxford: Blackwell.

Brown, R. (1973) *A First Language: The Early Stages*. Harmondsworth: Penguin.

Clark, E.V. (1973) 'What's in a word?' On the child's acquisition of semantics in his first language. In T.E. Moore (ed.), *Cognitive Development and the Acquisition of Language*. New York: Academic Press.

Clark, E.V. (1993) *The Lexicon in Acquisition*. Cambridge: Cambridge University Press.

Clark, H.H. and Clark, E.V. (1977) *Psychology and Language*. New York: Harcourt Brace Jovanovich.

Cruttenden, A. (1979) *Language in Infancy and Childhood*. Manchester: Manchester University Press.

Crystal, D. (1987) *Child Language, Learning and Linguistics: An Overview for the Teaching and Therapeutic Professions*. 2nd edn. London: Edward Arnold.

DeCasper, A.J. and Fifer, W.P. (1980) Of human bonding: newborns prefer their mothers' voices. *Science*, 208, 1174–6.

Eimas, P.D., Siqueland, E.R., Jusczyk, P.W. and Vigorito, J. (1971) Speech perception in infants. *Science*, 209, 1140–1 OR 171, 303–6.

Halliday, M.A.K. (1975) *Learning How to Mean: Explorations in the Development of Language*. London: Edward Arnold.

Ingram, D. (1989) *First Language Acquisition: Method, Description and Explanation*. Cambridge: Cambridge University Press.

Jusczck, P.W. (1997) *The Discovery of Spoken Language*. Cambridge, MA: MIT Press.

Kuhl, P.K. (1986) Theoretical contributions of tests on animals to the special-mechanisms debate in speech. *Journal of Experimental Biology*, 45(3), 233–65.

Kuhl, P.K. (1991) Perception, cognition, and ontogenetic and phylogenetic emergence of human speech. In S.E. Brauth, W.S. Hall and R.J. Dooling (eds), *Plasticity of Development*. Cambridge, MA: MIT Press, 73–106.

Ladefoged, P. (2004) *Vowels and Consonants: An Introduction to the Sounds of Language*. 2nd edn. Oxford: Blackwell.

Macrory, G. (2001) Language development: what do early years practitioners need to know? *Early Years: An International Journal of Research and Development*, 21(1), 33–40.

Mehler, J., Jusczyk, P.W., Lambertz, G., Halsted, N., Bertoncini, J. and Amiel-Tison, C. (1988) A precursor of language acquisition in young infants. *Cognition*, 29, 143–78.

Nelson, K. (1973) Structure and strategy in learning to talk. *Monographs of the Society for Research in Child Development*, serial no. 149, 38(1–2).

Pan, B. A. and Gleason J. B. (2001) Semantic Development: Learning the Meanings of Words. In Gleason, J. B. (ed.) *The Development of Language*. 5th edn. London: Allyn and Bacon.

Peccei, J.S. (1994) *Child Language*. London: Routledge.

Saxton, M. (2017) *Child Language*. 2nd edn. London: SAGE.

Tager-Flusberg, H. (ed.) (1994) *Constraints on Language Acquisition: Studies of Atypical Children*. Hove: Lawrence Erlbaum.

Vihman, M. (1996) *Phonological Development: The Origins of Language in the Child*. Oxford: Blackwell.

4

LATER LANGUAGE DEVELOPMENT: 5-11

INTRODUCTION

In this chapter, we are going to look at features of language and communication in later childhood and consider the implications for school and
classroom. We will pick up from some of the things we looked at in Chapter 3,
to see how they develop further as children go through the later years of
primary school. First of all, here is a quick recap on what children starting
school (Year 1, aged five, rising six) can do: pronounce all the vowels and
most of the consonants of their language(s), use some stress and intonation
appropriately, converse with some fluency using a range of grammatical
features, tenses, questions, negatives and so on. They can use language to
ask, answer, explain, describe, speculate and entertain – to name just a few
purposes for which they can talk. As a conversationalist, a five-year-old can
actively participate in talk with adults and other children, take turns and
maintain the topic of conversation. The average five-year-old may have a
vocabulary of several thousand words. Indeed, Nippold (2007: 22) suggests

that they know the meanings of some 10,000 words. It is not surprising that those who have followed the development of a child from birth are often amazed at the progress that they have made. It can (almost) appear that they have learned all that they need in order to communicate, so impressive can a conversation with a five-year-old be!

FURTHER LANGUAGE DEVELOPMENT

PHONOLOGY

Yet there remain various areas in which there is still important development to take place. Take **phonology** first of all: the pronunciation of some sounds is still not secure, notably fricatives such as /f/ and /θ/ (and, of course, in some regions /f/ and /θ/ are not distinguished – note the child who wrote that she had 'free fish' – meaning three!). This has implications for the development of phonemic awareness which is in turn crucial for the acquisition of literacy. Furthermore, some children may still be hearing differences at a sub-phonemic level, such as the nine-year-old child who told me that 'chicken' began with /t/ – which of course it does, the affricate / t ʃ/ being in initial position. Indeed, many people would struggle with the idea that 'chicken' starts with /t/ but it does! Other aspects of phonology are also important, such as stress at word and at sentence level. At **word level**, differences between compound words, such as blackbird, and noun phrases composed of adjective and noun, such as black bird, are very subtle. Similarly, there are numerous words spelled the same but with different stress according to their grammatical status – for example, when present is a noun the stress is on the first syllable; when a verb, the second. At **sentence level**, English is able to move the stress up and down the sentence. Take a sentence like 'I didn't know you were here' and say it several times, putting the stress on a different word every time. Unlike many other languages which have to change the grammar to change the meaning (French, for example), English can do it just with the stress.

A further aspect of phonology is that of **intonation**, which is used to signal all kinds of attitudes and expectations, such as surprise, doubt and so on. **Tag questions** have a particular role to play in English, as the same tag delivered with different intonation can convey quite different messages. On the one hand, a question such as 'you are going to make the dinner, aren't you?' can convey the expectation of 'yes' if delivered with a falling intonation on the tag. On the other hand, a rising intonation suggests much more of a genuine query. These are subtleties that young children starting school have not yet mastered and will take several further years to gain full control over. Similarly, **sarcasm** and **irony** are later acquired and children will often be perplexed by a comment such as 'that's nice' when the opposite meaning is intended by the speaker. One seven-year-old was listening to two teachers in the playground – one said she had found a dead bird on her doorstep, to which her colleagues replied, 'oh, that's nice'. The puzzled child immediately wanted to know what was nice about it.

LEXICAL DEVELOPMENT

Lexical development is also important. We have noted the expansion of vocabulary that takes place and young children's repertoires can be quite impressive. But as they move into the five to ten age range this will gather pace as new experiences and understandings bring more words. At this stage too children are developing literacy skills and the world of books brings them into contact with vocabulary beyond their immediate experience. This is one of many reasons for children to engage with literature, both fiction and non-fiction. Indeed, Stoel-Gammon (2011) estimates that six-year-old children have a vocabulary of 6,000 words, and children may learn between six and ten words a day between the ages of six and ten (see Saxton, 2017: 161). It is, of course, a difficult task to estimate precisely how many words a child has, as there will be differences between comprehension and production. In addition, this is not a simple matter of counting words. This is because vocabulary/lexical development is more than the *quantity* of words acquired. As children's cognition develops, so too must the ways in which words relate to each other. First of all, they acquire a greater range of meanings so that seemingly simple words can suddenly pose a problem. These are sometimes known as **polysemous** terms – that is, words with more than one meaning (Nippold, 2016: 49). Consider this example:

Adult: *Her husband's got a chair at Lancaster so they're moving up there.*

Child (aged 10):   *Why don't they just bring it back here?*

So much world knowledge is often needed to make sense of the language they hear, in this case the abstract meaning of professorship. The primary meaning, as in the example just offered, is often concrete and the secondary term more abstract. This does not apply only to nouns, of course. Prepositions such as *up, down, high, low* and *above* have physical meanings as well as non-physical: compare *the high shelf* to *she hit a high note*. It has indeed been noted that children have difficulties with such terms in the curriculum area of music and also in mathematics (Durkin *et al.*, 1986). Again, compare *go up the stairs* and *add these numbers up*. Unsurprisingly, young children find the abstract meanings of polysemous words harder to comprehend; this is something that develops with age. However, as Durkin *et al.* point out (1986: 93), this may mainly be a school-related phenomenon as it arises when children encounter particular areas of the curriculum. Be that as it may, an awareness of potential difficulties with apparently simple words can serve a teacher well. As we saw in Chapter 2, other words also have different kinds of meanings, sometimes known as double-function words (Nippold, 2016: 52). They may have both physical and psychological properties – words such as *hard, cold* or *sweet* can have both. So a cake or a drink can be sweet (as in sugary), but we can also call a person sweet. Research suggests that young children aged about three or four struggle with the non-literal meaning of the words. An early experiment by Asch and Nerlove (1960) interviewing children aged from three to twelve years, showed a gradual development over the age range, and they concluded that the ability to understand the physical meanings was several years ahead of the ability to understand the psychological ones.

RELATIONSHIPS BETWEEN WORDS

This is another potentially problematic area. Words have **synonyms** (same or similar meanings) and **antonyms** (opposites). Children can be quite amusing and inventive in their initial understandings and differ from each other. As explained previously in Chapter 2, one five-year-old we know thought that the opposite of *real* was *plastic*, whereas another child of a similar age informed us that the opposite of *real* was *pretend*. It is all too easy to assume that children invest these words with the meanings that adults have for them. A further aspect of the complex relationship between words is the issue of **superordinates**. A word like 'bird' is a superordinate; other words such as robin, starling and magpie are all examples of birds. But while every robin is a bird, not every bird is a robin, of course, so the relationship is only in one direction. A further issue is words that are on a **continuum of meaning**, such as adverbs of *magnitude* and *likelihood* (Nippold, 2007). Adverbs of magnitude include words such as *very, slightly, rather, quite* and so on. Adverbs of likelihood are words such as *possibly, probably* and *definitely*. As adult users of the language, it is easy to assume that the subtle gradations in meaning are understood by children. Finally, there is **deixis**. Some words change their meaning according to time and/ or place, for example: I/you, here/there, this/that.

FIGURATIVE LANGUAGE

A further issue is what we call **figurative** language. Language is rife with metaphors, similes, idioms, slang and ambiguous language such as irony and sarcasm. We noted above in the section on phonology that the subtle difference in intonation signals sarcasm or irony. Other kinds of figurative language such as metaphors and similes see a gradual increase in comprehension as children move through the school years. Similes are more transparent than metaphors, in that they use *like* or *as* to make a direct comparison, as *he fought like a lion*. In comparison, metaphors state that one thing *is* another thing, equating those two things not because they actually are the same, but for the sake of comparison or symbolism. As children mature, they become more capable of abstract thought. In order to understand metaphors, children need to have an awareness of the relevant semantic features of the words used. For example, to comprehend *he was a tiger in the fight* children need to have a grasp of the features of a tiger (strong, powerful, energetic) and of what is entailed in a fight (combat, winning or losing, strength). These are more common in the language than we might think. But children also can make sense of metaphors more easily if there are concrete rather than abstract nouns involved, and also where there is helpful linguistic context.

A final consideration is pointed out by Nippold (2007), who reminds us that there is an individual trajectory in lexical development, particularly once children can read independently. So a child with a particular interest in, for example, horses and horse riding will develop a different set of lexical items from the child who is very keen on the planetary system.

GRAMMAR

MORPHOLOGY

And there is still a way to go to master the **syntax** and the **morphology** of the language. As you would expect, there are several aspects to this. First of all, there are aspects of **morphology** to consider. We saw in Chapter 2 that we can think of morphology as **inflectional** or **derivational**. Recall that inflectional morphology (or grammatical morphology) is also what we might think of as 'grammatical inflections': the plural –s, the past tense –ed, the progressive –ing and so on. Most children do master inflectional morphology by around six or seven years of age, but plurals and verb tenses may still cause problems for children who continue to produce words such as *bringed* and *mouses*. So also do past participles, such that examples such as *tooken* and *drinken* persist until well into the second half of the primary school years. However, there is a relatively small set of these inflectional morphemes and many of children's errors will be to do with lack of familiarity with irregular forms. However, derivational morphology takes much longer to master and the acquisition of competence in this area will take until adolescence or even later. This is because there are so many affixes, more than 100 in English (Nippold, 2007: 49–50), including prefixes like un–, anti–, mis–, pre– and suffixes such as –tion, –ive, –ship and –tude. Children have to understand the meanings embedded in suffixes and prefixes. The school curriculum will bring many examples of morphologically complex words, often in written form, and the ability to understand these is crucial to academic success.

Clearly there is a difference between receptive and productive competence. Research suggests that receptive tasks are much easier than productive ones. In terms of production, target forms that are obviously linked to the original word (e.g. drive/driver) are easier for children than those that are what is called non-neutral (with a phonetic change). For example, long/length presents greater difficulty (Nippold, 2007: 57). Nippold further notes evidence pointing to a relationship between word knowledge and derivational morphology in young children, with the period of greatest development appearing to be between nine and fourteen years. This is aided by exposure to written academic language at school; children will begin to see the relationships between words, creating what we might call 'word families'. So, for example, they may start to see the relationship between *tolerate, tolerance, toleration, intolerable* and so on. Furthermore, knowledge of affixes can enable children to guess at the meaning of new words, encouraging independence. Thus a child who comes across a word such as *centurion* may recognise the common root of related words such as the *cent* in *century*.

SYNTAX

In this section, we will consider some of the aspects of syntax that continue to develop after the age of five. We saw in Chapter 2 that there are different kinds of sentences – simple, compound and complex. Let us recall that compound sentences require coordinating conjunctions 'and', 'but' or 'or', whereas the development of **complex sentences**, which have a main and a subordinate clause, requires mastery of a range of subordinating conjunctions, which link the two clauses together. These include *when, while, before, after, until, if, because, although* and, unsurprisingly, children will learn, for example, conjunctions such as *when* and *because* (often *'cos* in children's speech!) before, say, *although*. We also saw in Chapter 2 that subordinate clauses can be finite or non-finite. Therefore, mastery of these complex sentences is by no means complete by the age of five.

Within the sentence, however, elements at phase level also become more complicated. Again, in Chapter 2, we saw how a lengthy sentence can nevertheless still be a simple sentence. The example we used was 'the big fat fluffy white rabbits have been eating long juicy organic carrots'. Although this is a simple sentence (subject, verb, object), the **noun phrases** in subject and object position are long – 'the big fat fluffy white rabbits' is the subject and the object is 'long juicy organic carrots'. Equally, the verb phase 'have been eating' adds to the length and processing difficulty of the sentence. Within the **verb phrase**, auxiliary verbs are still problematic and may be missed, as in 'I making a seat for him' (age six). As late as age ten, modal verbs can be tricky – for example, 'It'll would be a funny colour' – as can phrasal verbs, such as 'you pick up it' (age seven). We noted in Chapter 3 that modal auxiliaries (e.g. can, could, shall, should, must, may and might) are later to develop. This is partly because they involve more complex concepts. They are, however, vital aspects of the language to develop as they allow speculation, reflection and so on. Without being able to say what *might* happen, predicting the possible outcome of a science activity is impossible. Even more complex is talking about what didn't happen but could have happened (or not). A sentence like, *if it hadn't rained, we could have gone to the park* is a complex construction (note that when learning a foreign language, this type of construction will be at an advanced stage). But even more so is turning this into a question: *if it hadn't rained, could we have gone to the park?* As we saw in Chapter 3, four-year-olds do produce these, albeit not necessarily correctly or consistently. In a school context, therefore, children need the opportunity to hear such questions and to answer them (and to ask them) – for example, in an art lesson, *if we had mixed green and blue, what colour might it have made?*

Some questions can be difficult too, with children at times marking past tense twice: 'did you counted that one?' (age eight). This is unsurprising as, in English, once we introduce the auxiliary 'do' the past tense ending is no longer needed (see Chapter 2). Tag questions have already been mentioned with regard to intonation but can also be difficult grammatically: 'it could be a bungalow, couldn't he?' (age twelve). The rules for tag questions in English are essentially that they enjoy what is called a reversal of polarity (Perera, 1984: 34).

She will go, won't she?

She won't go, will she?

However, it is also possible to use these without reverse polarity, as in, for example: *we're having a party, are we?* Compare this with *we're having a party, aren't we?* There is a subtle difference of meaning, further nuanced by the intonation used.

Equally, there are aspects of **negation** that pose problems, although some are more likely to be encountered in more formal and/or written language. As illustrated above, the combination of modal auxiliaries and negatives (and then turned into a question!) is challenging. The following examples illustrate some possible issues in more formal written language:

The day was neither warm nor sunny.

If only he had known, the bus was on its way.

She was anything but happy.

In all these examples it is not instantly clear what the negative is as, essentially, the negation is concealed. Equally in these next examples where there are two clauses, it is not clear in the first one that there is a negative as the second clause read or heard alone may give the opposite impression. They both end in the same way despite the fact that in one sentence the teacher is angry and in the other she isn't!

It was not true that the teacher was angry.

She didn't know that the teacher was angry.

A further grammatical element to consider is the use of **passives**. Just within this one area, children face several different aspects that must be mastered. Some passives are full (e.g. he was hit by the ball), whereas others are truncated (e.g. he was hit); another issue is that some statements in the passive are non-reversible and others are reversible. Thus those that are reversible ('the boy was hit by the girl' could equally be the other way round and make sense) may be more likely to be misunderstood than those where the reverse relationship is unlikely (the cake was enjoyed by all the family).

PRAGMATICS

Another very important aspect of later language development is **pragmatics**. While this is part of language development from very early on, there remains much to be learned in the school years. Adopting the appropriate register for their audience is gradually learned, as they come to realise that 'shut that door' might need to be rephrased for certain audiences. In later language development, an important aspect of pragmatics is learning to appreciate the other person's social perspective – that is, their listener's state of mind. This is vital in order to know what topic can be discussed with whom, what is socially appropriate (and this is culturally constrained – for example, in some cultures it is considered impolite to ask someone how much they earn, in others this is quite acceptable) and the extent to which the listener is already knowledgeable about the topic. Children's conversational skills thus develop considerably during the school years as they learn how to stay on topic and how to carefully change topic, known as topic shading (Nippold, 2016: 215). Not only is earning to take your turn in a conversation tricky, but learning how to interrupt is trickier still! Equally, to be a good conversationalist, learning how to listen is crucial. This requires a number of skills, including, for example, showing that one is paying attention, how to seek clarification or request further detail. This awareness of audience is extremely important to effective communication, so choosing the right register for your listener(s) is vital.

Children in upper primary school may already be beginning to adopt elements of an **adolescent register**. Adolescents and teenagers are often criticised in the popular press for their use of language, but in fact they are usually developing a register that they use in tandem with other registers already developed. While they may at times deliberately use their adolescent register in an inappropriate context to be provocative or confrontational, this in fact actually reflects a grasp of the sociolinguistic elements of language! This adolescent register is an important way to mark membership of a social group, and can change rapidly. It either falls out of fashion or is absorbed into the general lexicon – in which case, typically, it is abandoned by young people who then create new words and meanings.

As children go out into the world beyond the home, they also become more aware of other **accents** and **dialects**, and often approximate those of their peers rather than their parents. Children typically arrive at school with the dialect of their local area and/or family. Every language has a range of dialects, meaning that there are differences at the lexical and grammatical level. At the lexical level, many words have a huge number of variants across the country. An oft noted example is the many different words for bread rolls in the UK, such as *bap*, *barm* or *cob*. Grammar also differs according to dialect, so that, for example, in a northern English dialect, we can say, 'I was stood' at the bus stop and 'them books' whereas the dialect known as Standard English will use 'I was standing at the bus stop' and 'those books'. It should be stressed here that from a linguistic perspective, both dialects are equal. For historical reasons, Standard English attracts more social prestige than other dialects and competence in it is generally expected for social and economic success (see, for example, Fairclough, 2015). This is the dialect that children will encounter at school, particularly in formal written contexts. Thus they can extend their linguistic repertoire by becoming bi-dialectal. We should guard against the notion that dialects that are not Standard English are in some way inferior. Indeed, children whose local dialect happens to be Standard English can enjoy learning about other dialects through appropriate literature and contact with speakers. Standard English can, of course, be spoken in any accent, which is a different matter. Of course, there tends to be a co-occurrence of dialects and accents in many areas, such that a Scottish dialect is likely to be spoken with a Scottish accent.

EXTENDED DISCOURSE

Later language development involves grammar beyond the sentence, at the level of discourse. This involves coherence – the way content is held together (organised) and elaborated upon. It also crucially involves **cohesion**; this is the use of linguistic devices employed to link sentences together. This is done in a number of ways. Within extended discourse, there is use of **pronominal reference**, where pronouns are used as a reference to someone or something previously introduced. While repetition is also used as a cohesive device, substituting, for example, a name with a pronoun avoids excessive repetition but is a sophisticated skill. Children can be reprimanded for using a pronoun instead of a name! We noted above in the section on syntax that certain conjunctions used within the sentence are acquired before others. However, at the level of discourse, we need to think about how sentences or utterances are connected to one another.

Connectives are words or phrases that link sentences within a text. Key kinds of connectives are: adversative (e.g. *but, however, nevertheless, on the other hand*), additive (e.g. *and, furthermore, moreover*), temporal (e.g. *then, after*), causal (e.g. *because, consequently, as a result*). As such, connectives can link one sentence to a previous one within discourse. Words like 'however' are adversative (sometimes referred to as oppositional), but are likely to be acquired later than 'but'. This is true of all the kinds of connectives – for example, additive connectives such as 'moreover' will come later than 'and'. Some will be more common in certain types of written text. We will return to this point when we consider the development of narrative. A further cohesive device is **ellipsis**, which is learning what to omit, odd though this may sound. But as one child aged seven demonstrated, this is not obvious. On being told that her father would be home between 'seven and half past', she asked 'half past what?' And this varies from language to language. For example, in English, we can say 'I ran home and ate my dinner', whereas in French the pronoun 'I' has to be repeated before 'ate'. **Lexical cohesion** is the use of different lexical items to refer to the same person or thing. In *George's Marvellous Medicine*, author Roald Dahl refers to the grandma in a number of ways – in the same paragraph, she is 'Grandma', 'that horrid old witchy woman' and 'this old woman'. This happens just as much in spoken language as in written, but context may enable the listener to make sense of what is being said. Discourse, of course, operates with both spoken and written language alike. However, the context often fills in the 'gaps' in spoken language and, in addition, the person the child is interacting with can spot a lack of comprehension and try to repair the communication. However, cohesion on its own is insufficient. It relates to the micro-level of the text – that is, the words and sentences and how they join together. Texts must also be *coherent*. This means that ideas must be organised and connected in ways that can be understood, and this concerns, therefore, the *macro*-level features of a text, such as the way the theme is introduced and maintained and devices such as summarising and recapping.

So far, we have largely considered the development of dialogue and conversation. But children must also develop the ability to construct a piece of language that could be a 'stand-alone' or a monologue, known also as 'decontextualised language' (Ely, 2001: 422). The ability to do this will have obvious implications for the acquisition of written language, particularly for the kind required in school settings. Furthermore, connected text, whether spoken or written, will vary according to the genre of language. **Narratives** constitute one genre widely studied in children and unsurprisingly show a developmental trajectory. Narratives are frequent in both spoken and written language, and conversations often include story- or anecdote-telling. Narrative (in its broadest sense) is perhaps the most common form of extended discourse (Karmiloff-Smith, 1986: 269). Children from an early age engage with this, but typically switch between past and present at preschool age, but only later learn to stick to past tense. In a study by Berman and Slobin (1994), in different languages, the three- to four-year-olds tended to switch between present and past in describing the events depicted in a picture book, whereas older children, increasingly from age five years up, demonstrated a narrative storytelling mode by adhering to mostly past-tense forms. Narrative, of course, needs the kind of cohesive devices outlined above, but the development of these continues well beyond middle childhood (Berman, 2015), the earliest marked being 'and'. All those who work with young children will have noted the way in which they will tell a tale with 'and' … 'and' … 'and' …! We earlier mentioned pronominal reference, but reference itself is a broader concept, something we as adults take for granted, referring to other things, events and people. However, as Berman (2015: 467) points out, reference is cognitively demanding, requiring later-developing abilities such as memory retention across stretches of discourse, grasp of the distinction between new and given information, understanding of mutual knowledge and the ability to provide sufficient, but non-redundant, information about who or what is being referred to at each point. As she says 'coordinating all these facets of information processing while also encoding them by appropriate linguistic means is a formidable task for children, even at school age'. We should also note here that there is a clear link not just with cognitive development, but also pragmatic development, as outlined earlier in this chapter. This is also true of other genres, such as explanation and description, which must be mastered by children.

DIFFERENCES BETWEEN SPOKEN AND WRITTEN LANGUAGE

While this book is primarily about learning to *talk*, we cannot ignore the fact that the primary school years bring children into contact with the written language – indeed this happens earlier in early childhood care settings and in the home. Thus, we need to ask ourselves if there are differences between these modes of language. Spoken language is often thought of as contextualised and indeed it often is, embedded in context that enables understanding and in dialogue or conversation offering opportunities to repair, clarify or make additions. However, it can also be lacking in context, or with reduced context. For example, turning on the radio when speakers are in the middle of a debate can often throw us as we are initially without any context. This is quite different to planning to listen to a particular item, perhaps thinking about it in advance and bring to mind what we know already about the topic. Much written language is decontextualised, especially in a school setting. It is a huge jump from contextualised informal speech to, for example, writing an expository piece explaining a topic for an audience, using the linguistic features appropriate to the genre. However, while written language is generally considered to be decontextualised, this may be a matter of degree rather than an absolute – think of the recipe with the accompanying photograph and the familiar lay out. It can also be interactive, as in the participation in a WhatsApp group conversation or a text exchange. Indeed, the tendency for many to say they have been 'speaking' or 'talking' to someone when in fact they were producing written texts underlines the way in which this resembles an oral exchange. As Barton and Lee (2011: 600) point out, 'although they have different properties, written and spoken language are not easy to separate in actual use'. Nevertheless, they go on to say that 'written language has a life of its own … It does not just amplify spoken language. It extends the functions of language, and enables us to do different things.'

Having said that, children will bring their spoken language to the task, and early writing may display some of the grammatical features of spoken language. There are a number of features exclusive to informal spoken language (see Perera, 1984). For example, the use of indefinite reference as 'I saw this man at the bus stop' is using 'this' in a quite different way to saying 'I want this book', meaning a specific (definite) book. The use of 'this' and 'these' for indefinite reference is very common in spoken language. Another feature is what is called the recapitulatory pronoun, as in, 'our postman, he's really nice'. Another is the amplificatory noun phrase tag, as in 'she's nice, your mum'. And there are clause completers such as 'and that', 'and all'. The spoken language will often use the verb 'to get' rather than 'to be' as, typically, we will say things such as 'he got run over'. Another feature of informal spoken language is the tendency to use the verb 'to go' in place of 'to say', as in, for example, when relating some tale, 'so she went … and he went …'. A relative newcomer is the quotative 'be like' for reported speech and thought, although Romaine and Lange (1991) give examples from American English as long ago as the 1980s, as in 'And she's LIKE, "Um … Well, that's cool" ' (Romaine and Lange, 1991: 227). Not only is it very common in British English and other varieties (Tagliamonte and Hudson, 1999; Tagliamonte and D'Arcy, 2004), but, intriguingly, similar ways of reporting speech exist in other languages (Cheshire and Secova, 2018). Many, if not all, of these features of spoken language are in such common usage that you may not even be aware of them. If you haven't noticed some of these before it is an interesting exercise to listen out for them! So how does written language differ? Space does not permit a comprehensive overview, but even in young children's story books, there are word order differences, such as 'at the end of the lane was a small cottage', with the subject of the sentence at the end rather than the beginning. More formal texts may have lengthy noun phrases in subject position and nominalisation is often found. This is where a spoken utterance such as 'when the train arrived …', using a verb phrase, can be phrased in writing as 'on the arrival of the train'. The use of the passive is also more frequent, as in 'when asked about the new policy, the minister said …'. Another task for the teacher is to develop the skills of analysing the features that characterise various written texts. And, of course, in addition to differences in syntax and the organisation of different types of text at discourse level, there is the increasing exposure to more abstract words and concepts as children go through the school years. As this develops, there is a reciprocal relationship between spoken and written language, as the lexis and syntax of formal written language will enhance spoken communicative competence, thus expanding the spoken linguistic repertoire as well as developing literacy skills. Importantly, however, there is abundant evidence that children's oracy skills are closely related to their development of literacy (for a review, see Jones, 2017), making the development of spoken language fundamental to school success.

METALINGUISTIC AWARENESS: WHAT IS IT?

A final consideration for this chapter is the development of metalinguistic awareness – that is, the ability to think about and reflect upon the nature and functions of language (Pratt and Grieve, 1984) and see it as separate from the things it represents. This means the ability to focus one's attention on the language itself, rather than the meaning. However, this is not a single uniform concept as it requires multiple skills at different levels of language: phonological, morphological, syntactic and lexical (Bialystok *et al.*, 2014). Indeed, Gombert (1992) distinguishes between metaphonological, metalexical, metasemantic, metasyntactic and metapragmatic awareness. So it is one thing to become aware of, say, the syllables of the language, another to judge whether something is grammatically correct or pragmatically appropriate.

Ely (2001: 423) suggests that a precursor to metalinguistic awareness may be when children self-correct, but notes that this may be simply that they implicitly recognise a difference between their speech and the model they have heard. Ely argues that true metalinguistic awareness of the language system is explicit. How long does this take? In terms of metasemantic awareness, for example, Ely notes that children between the ages of five and seven can recognise words like *dog* as 'words', but struggle with function words like *the*. Children's awareness of pragmatics develops through childhood and by the end of primary school usually they can be expected to understand the rules. A key moment is often when they begin to appreciate jokes and double meanings, around the age of seven – and they are often relentless in telling joke after joke! We noted above the tendency of adolescents to use an inappropriate register deliberately – which also clearly suggests strong metalinguistic awareness. Phonological awareness develops generally by the age of seven, with most children able to segment words. The exposure to literacy in school, particularly where there is explicit attention paid to segmentation (syllables, consonant and vowels), has a hastening effect upon the development of metalinguistic skills. Indeed, Gombert (1992) is of the view that explicit awareness, particularly with syntax, requires formal education in literacy skills. Metasyntactic awareness, then, will develop in tandem with learning to read and write. A final issue to consider, albeit briefly, is when it is appropriate to expect children to use metalinguistic *terminology* and label concepts such as nouns and verbs. The National Curriculum in England (DfE, 2014) sets out clear expectations in this regard, and there is no doubt that being able to talk about one's writing, for example, or a foreign language can be helpful. However, care is needed to ensure that this is done in a contextualised and age-appropriate way, and teacher knowledge of both language and effective pedagogy is of great importance (see, for example, Myhill *et al.*, 2012). However, as Myhill and Watson (2014) note, simply teaching grammar as the isolated naming and labelling of word classes and syntactical structures is of little obvious benefit. Rather, they see a role for grammar in the writing curriculum as a functionally oriented endeavour, developing students' metalinguistic thinking and decision-making in writing.

CHAPTER SUMMARY

This chapter has reviewed the development of spoken language in later childhood, aiming to illustrate the extent of development still to take place across a number of domains. While some of these may appear to be less of a 'milestone' than some earlier steps such as first words, the very subtlety and complexity of these later developments require just as much attention. What we see is an expansion of linguistic repertoire across multiple domains, as the child becomes an ever more effective speaker at the same time as taking steps into the world of written language. What is absolutely crucial, however, is that we do not allow the world of reading and writing to overshadow the oral skills on which they initially depend, but that we also see the need to ensure that spoken language continues to flourish.

REFERENCES

Asch, S.E. and Nerlove, H. (1960) The development of double-function words in children: an exploratory investigation. In B. Kaplan and S. Wapner (eds), *Perspectives in Psychological Theory: Essays in Honor of Heinz Werner*. New York: International Universities Press.

Barton, D. and Lee, C. (2011) Literacy studies. In R. Wodak (ed.), *The SAGE Handbook of Sociolinguistics*. London: SAGE.

Berman, R.A. (2015) Language development and use beyond the sentence. In E. Bavin, L. Naigles and R. Letitia (eds) *The Cambridge Handbook of Child Language*. 2nd edn. Cambridge: Cambridge University Press.

Berman, R.A. and Slobin, D.I. (1994) *Relating Events in Narrative: A Crosslinguistic Developmental Study*. Hillsdale, NJ: Erlbaum.

Bialystok, E., Peets, K.F. and Moreno, S. (2014) Producing bilinguals through immersion education: development of metalinguistic awareness. *Applied Psycholinguistics*, 35, 177–91.

Cheshire, J. and Secova, M. (2018) The origins of new quotative expressions: the case of Paris French. *Journal of French Language Studies*, 28, 209–34.

Department for Education (DfE) (2014) *National Curriculum in England*. Available at: https://www.gov.uk/government/collections/national-curriculum

Durkin, K., Crowther, R.D. and and Shire, B. (1986) Children's processing of polysemous vocabulary in school. In K. Durkin (ed.), *Language Development in the School Years*. London: Croom Helm.

Ely, R. (2001) Language and literacy in the school years. In J.B. Gleason (ed.), *The Development of Language*. 5th edn. London: Allyn and Bacon.

Fairclough, N. (2015) *Language and Power*. 3rd edn. London: Routledge.

Gombert, J.E. (1992) *Metalinguistic Development*. London: Harvester Wheatsheaf.

Jones, D. (2017) Talking about talk: reviewing oracy in English primary education. *Early Child Development and Care*, 187(3–4), 498–508.

Karmiloff-Smith, A. (1986) Some fundamental aspects of language development after age 5. In P. Fletcher and M. Garman (eds), *Language Acquisition*. 2nd edn. Cambridge: Cambridge University Press.

Myhill, D.A. and Watson, A. (2014) The role of grammar in the writing curriculum: a review of the literature. *Child Language Teaching and Therapy*, 30(1), 41–62.

Myhill, D.A., Jones, S.M., Lines, H. and Watson, A. (2012) Re-thinking grammar: the impact of embedded grammar teaching on students' writing and students' metalinguistic understanding. *Research Papers in Education*, 27(2), 139–66.

Nippold, M.A. (2007) *Later Language Development: School-Age Children, Adolescents, and Young Adults*. 3rd edn. Austin, TX: Pro-Ed. Inc.

Nippold, M.A. (2016) *Later Language Development: School-Age Children, Adolescents, and Young Adults*. 4th edn. Austin, TX: Pro-Ed. Inc.

Perera, K. (1984) *Children's Writing and Reading*. Oxford: Blackwell.

Pratt, C. and Grieve, R. (1984) The development of metalinguistic awareness: an introduction. In W.E. Tunmer, C. Pratt and M.L. Herriman (eds), *Metalinguistic Awareness in Children*. Springer Series in Language and Communication, vol. 15. Berlin, Heidelberg: Springer. https://doi.org/10.1007/978-3-642-69113-3_1

Romaine, S.R. and Lange, D. (1991) The use of like as a marker of reported speech and thought: a case of grammaticalization in progress. *American Speech*, 66(3), 227–79.

Saxton, M. (2017) *Child Language*. 2nd edn. London: SAGE.

Stoel-Gammon, C. (2011) Relationships between lexical and phonological development in young children. *Journal of Child Language*, 38, 1–34.

Tagliamonte, S. and D'Arcy, A. (2004) He's like, she's like: the quotative system in Canadian youth. *Journal of Sociolinguistics*, 8(4), 493–514.

Tagliamonte, S. and Hudson, R. (1999) Be like et al. beyond America: the quotative system in British and Canadian youth. *Journal of Sociolinguistics*, 3(2), 147–72.

PART III

LEARNING MORE THAN ONE LANGUAGE

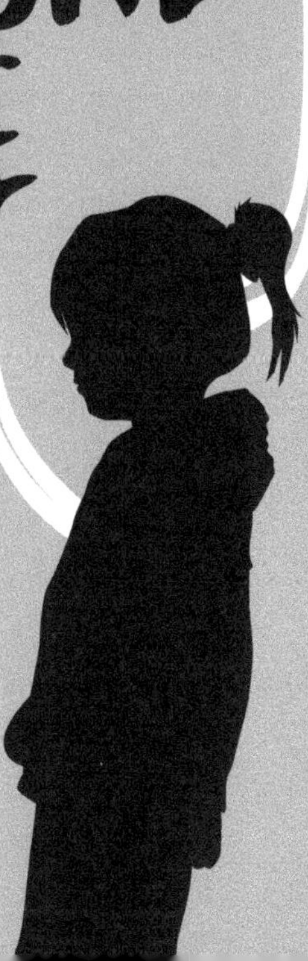

5

THE BILINGUAL CHILD: SIMULTANEOUS BILINGUALISM

In the last chapter, I introduced the idea that children are developing a linguistic *repertoire*. In many classrooms, from nursery upwards, this repertoire will extend far beyond English, given the number of children whose upbringing has been bilingual or plurilingual. We use the term **plurilingual** to describe an individual's use of several languages, whereas the term **multilingual** tends to refer to the context. This means that in many schools, students arrive in your classroom with more than one language at their disposal. This should not surprise us. What does often surprise those new to the study of multilingualism, however, is the global context of language learning and use. The latest edition of *Ethnologue* reports 7,117 languages currently in use. Of course, some are much more widely used than others (see Coulmas, 2018) and we could squabble in some cases as to whether a language variant is a 'language' or a 'dialect'. Having said that, we need to take into account the fact that there are only just under 200 countries or nation states in the world. Of course, this is a number that alters from time to time – once we considered the former Yugoslavia to be one country whereas now there are several Balkan countries in the same territory. Nevertheless, even allowing for possible fluctuations, and the fact that some languages have millions of speakers and others very few, we are left with the inescapable conclusion that with 200 countries and 7,000+ languages, we live in a multilingual, multicultural world. And every one of those languages is as complex and rich as the languages you, the reader, speak. It is easy to lose perspective on this in the UK, given the global status of English and the number of monolingual speakers here. While there is no doubting the prevalence of English in many countries and its use around the world in commerce, banking, science and so on, we need to challenge the notion that 'everyone speaks English'. They do not. In fact, about 75 per cent of the world's population speak no English at all. And while the remaining approximately 25 per cent do speak English, more people learn it as a second or foreign language than as a first language (Crystal, 2004: 14). Thus many speakers of English are not monolingual speakers of it, but have it as part of their plurilingual repertoire, learned either from birth or acquired later in life. Within the UK, many speakers are indeed bi- or plurilingual, speaking more than 300 languages in London alone (Panayi, 2020). Some, however, might question whether there are in fact truly monolingual language users. Most people will have recourse to more than one dialect, and even within one dialect there are registers, so speakers are constantly adjusting to audience and drawing upon their linguistic repertoire.

In the case of bilingual or plurilingual speakers, this linguistic repertoire contains more than one language. Such speakers will often among themselves switch between the different languages they speak – this is often referred to as code-switching. This can happen in a number of ways such as half way through a conversation, or even mid-sentence. A more recent perspective sees this as translanguaging, which rejects the conception of bilingualism as parallel monolingualisms (Heller, 2007). In other words, the two languages are not seen as separate 'codes'; rather, the speaker is simply drawing upon the full linguistic repertoire at their disposal, according to context. This is an important feature of language use that we need to keep in mind, particularly as we consider a rather pervasive myth.

TYPES OF BILINGUALISM

Before we do, let us first of all make a distinction between **simultaneous** bilingualism and **consecutive** bilingualism. On the one hand, simultaneous bilingualism (or plurilingualism) refers to a situation where the child is exposed to more than one language from birth. On the other hand, consecutive (or successive) bilingualism refers to the situation whereby the child is not exposed to the other language(s) from birth but acquires them later. What do we mean by later? McLaughlin (1984) suggests that age three is an appropriate cut-off point, given the amount of progress already made in one language by this stage in development. He acknowledges that this is arbitrary, but suggests that after age three children can no longer be considered to be acquiring the languages simultaneously. Meisel (2008), following the 'critical period hypothesis' proposed by Lenneberg back in 1967 (that is, the idea that there is a critical period for language learning, after which it is no longer possible), thinks that the age between three and four is crucial, especially for grammar (see Chapter 1). Some argue for a younger cut-off point, however. For example, de Houwer (1995: 222–3) suggests that the very early months are important – even a month after birth for first exposure to the second language (up to the age of two) makes a difference – and describes this as bilingual second language acquisition. This leaves us with the problem of how to describe children who fall in between these ages – for example, between one and four. Some researchers call these 'early successive bilinguals' (see Unsworth and Hulk, 2009: 70). While we need to acknowledge these different approaches, from a practitioner's perspective, however, perhaps the important thing is that many children arrive in nursery or reception (aged three or four) to some degree already bilingual. There may be an imbalance in the level of competence in the two languages, but we will nevertheless regard these children as having grown up as simultaneous bilinguals. Of course, there may be a difference between a child who has been exposed to two languages from birth and one who has encountered the new language at age two, but, as we shall see below, age is not by any means the only factor in this.

This means that bilingual or plurilingual children will have more than one language at their disposal – but does this cause confusion?

CONFUSED – MOI? DISPELLING THE MYTH

First of all, we should dispel a myth – that it is confusing for a child to learn more than one language. Children are not confused by multiple referents; they don't get confused by the fact that the person they know as 'daddy' is called 'Mike' by other people. Second, we are apt to see languages through an adult lens. We are socialised to see languages as discrete entities (French, Swahili, Mandarin), a concept reinforced by the association of particular languages with particular countries, further reinforced by the notion of countries having 'official' languages. However, very young children do not know that they are learning 'only' one language or indeed that they are learning more than one. They are simply learning language. We will consider shortly how they come to differentiate languages. In time they will need to use each language independently; a child growing up with, say, French and English can mix these and switch between them in a French–English-speaking home, but at some point may need to converse with speakers who only speak one of these languages, for example, English neighbours or French grandparents. Here, in fact, young children are learning how not to confuse *other* people! We have already seen how important the development of pragmatics is and that there is substantial evidence that young children are adept at tailoring their utterances to their audience. There is no reason to assume that this would be less the case with two or more languages. An anecdote I have reported elsewhere (Macrory, 2006) illustrates this nicely. My two-year-old PhD subject, Adèle, was reading with her father, whom she spoke to primarily in English. Sitting slightly apart from them, and unable to see the picture book, I must have looked puzzled by Adèle apparently saying the word 'scream'. This prompted her to get off her father's lap, bring me the book with a picture of an *ice* cream and tell me it was 'la glace' (French for ice cream). As I usually spoke French in their household, she clearly thought the problem was the English – not that she could necessarily have explained that. She was definitely not confused – and she was making sure I was not confused either!

WHAT DOES IT MEAN TO BE BILINGUAL?

The bilingual child or adult: perhaps in popular conceptions, this is the person who has a perfect command of both languages. Many people think of a bilingual family as consisting of two parents each with a different language, which is sometimes referred to as 'one person – one language'. Life, however, is rarely that simple as this is often not the case. Romaine (1995: 183–5) sets out six possible situations in which children may grow up bilingually, taking as variables the languages spoken by the parents, the language spoken by the community and the strategy adopted by the parents for speaking to the child. These are as follows:

Type 1: 'One person – one language'

Parents: The parents have different native languages with each having some degree of competence in the other's language.

Community: The language of one of the parents is the dominant language of the community.

Strategy: The parents each speak their own language to the child from birth.

Type 2: 'Non-dominant home language'/'One language – one environment'

Parents: The parents have different native languages.

Community: The language of one of the parents is the dominant language of the community.

Strategy: Both parents speak the non-dominant language to the child, who is fully exposed to the dominant language only when outside the home, and in particular in nursery school.

Type 3: 'Non-dominant home language without community support'

Parents: The parents share the same native language.

Community: The dominant language is not that of the parents.

Strategy: The parents speak their own language to the child.

Type 4: 'Double non-dominant home language without community support'

Parents: The parents have different native languages.

Community: The dominant language is different from either of the parents' languages.

Strategy: The parents each speak their own language to the child from birth.

Type 5: 'Non-native parents'

Parents: The parents share the same native language.

Community: The dominant language is the same as that of the parents.

Strategy: One of the parents always addresses the child in a language which is not his/her native language.

Type 6: 'Mixed languages'

Parents: The parents are bilingual.

Community: Sectors of community may also be bilingual.

Strategy: Parents code-switch and mix languages.

Adèle, my PhD subject, fell into Type 1. Her mother was French, her father English and the dominant language here in the UK also English. Her father understood and spoke some French and her mother spoke fluent English. However, she always addressed Adèle in French, the sole exception being when her mother-in-law was present, when she spoke English as a courtesy because her mother-in-law understood no French at all. Type 2 can be illustrated by the case of a family living in the UK, where the mother is English and the father Spanish-speaking, but who chose to interact in Spanish in the home to maximise the input to the child. This, of course, requires the parent who has English as a first language to have a degree of competence in the other language. The Type 3 scenario can arise when, for example, two Hungarian-speaking parents agree that the family language will be Hungarian, even though the dominant language outside the home is English. Type 4 is illustrated by Hoffman (1991), who describes the experience of bringing up her children trilingually in an English context, where she spoke German to them and their father Spanish. Type 5 is perhaps more unusual. Saunders (1988) brought up his children to be German–English bilinguals in Australia, despite the fact that neither he nor the mother were first language speakers of German. Finally, Type 6 may be where both parents are fully bilingual in say English and Mandarin, know many people who are also bilingual and both languages are used freely by both parents. These six scenarios may not even fully reflect the complexity of bilingual situations at home. For example, Deuchar and Quay (2000) report a case study of an English-speaking mother and a Spanish-speaking father both speaking Spanish at home but English outside the home, so that, for example, the mother spoke Spanish at breakfast but switched to English upon arrival at daycare (2000: 6).

The above now gives us some idea of how complex a bilingual family situation can be, and shows how variable the input can be. Yip (2013) stresses the importance of the quantity *and* quality of the input, arguing that the input plays a decisive role. Yet the variety of possible contexts means that it may be difficult to provide the same input in both languages – for example, where the Hungarian parents decide that the limited exposure the children will get to Hungarian means that this must take priority over English. It would in any case be counter-intuitive not to speak to each other in a shared first language. Thus, in situations such as this, children may not arrive in nursery or reception classes with both languages developed to the same degree. Romaine's different scenarios also illustrate the dilemma that parents may face when adopting a strategy. Early on, however, the literature about this was somewhat dominated by the 'one person – one language' (OPOL) strategy proposed by Ronjat in 1913, who found that his speaking to their child Louis in French and his wife in German resulted in a child who spoke both languages fluently. Equally, a well-known case study by Leopold (1949/1970) of his daughter Hildegard, who learned to speak German to her father but English to her mother, served to reinforce this message. But even in a situation that lends itself to this (e.g. Type 1 above), it is not without possible problems, such as Adèle's mother switching to English when her mother-in-law was present. And when the parents address each other, *someone* usually has to switch languages. Also, once a child starts school in a dominant English environment, this may result in the minority language taking a back seat, therefore needing more input and reinforcement at home.

Further issues to consider are **family structure** and **community**. Many publications focus on the role of parents, but it is important to look at the wider picture – for example, Kenner *et al.* (2004) report an intergenerational research project in east London, offering examples of how children learned from grandparents, such as learning the names of fruit and vegetables in Sylheti/Bengali while gardening. Siblings too have a part to play. Barron-Hauwert (2011) describes how her three children reacted differently to the French–English bilingual situation they were growing up in. She suggests that parents may need to adapt strategies according to the needs of different children, and that personality and birth order can affect children's individual linguistic histories. Furthermore, she discusses the language that siblings use with each other and suggests that children often make decisions about their preferred language independent of their parents' strategy; they often prefer the language of the school and community. This should not surprise us as children and teenagers are usually keen to fit in with their peer group. In addition, they are often introduced to particular activities in the language of school or playground and then use that with each other, such as playing games in the school language even at home but speaking the other language with parents at meal times. Furthermore, beyond the family, many children attend what we call either supplementary or complementary schools, which can play a key role in developing children's rich linguistic resources (Kenner and Ruby, 2012: 3). As Conteh (2007) points out, in such schools the teachers are often bi- or plurilingual (unlike many teachers in mainstream schools).

The linguistic worlds that bilingual children experience, then, are complex environments. Grosjean (2013) offers as a definition of bilingualism the use of two or more languages (or dialects) in everyday life, but he makes a distinction between fluency and use. He argues that while fluency is important, it is equally pressing to understand how frequently bilingual speakers use their languages. Not only this – we need to know in which domains (situations) bilingual speakers use their languages and how modalities differ (speaking, reading, listening, writing) (2013: 9). If we think about young children growing up bilingually, it may be that in certain situations they always are exposed to and use one language. This can happen very easily, especially if parents adopt roles such as one parent always taking the child to the supermarket or giving the child a bath. Grosjean goes on to point out that languages 'wax and wane' as use fluctuates. An example already alluded to is when the child starts school and the balance of language use alters in favour of the dominant language. However, he also points out that there is a relationship between domains and fluency, suggesting that the more domains in which a language is used, the greater the fluency; conversely, if a language is used in only a few situations, the speaker will have less opportunity to develop fluency. If there is a domain in which one of the languages is never used, the speaker may not develop the vocabulary or the language style needed (2013: 12). A further issue, of course, is whether the child or adult is what is sometimes referred to as a passive or active bilingual; in other words, there may be words or turns of phrase which are recognised but not readily accessible to produce. The context thus is very important because this is what offers the input and the opportunities for interaction that the child will need for both languages to develop. In Chapter 1, we saw the important role of input and interaction in language development. This can only be more important in the case of developing more than one language.

BILINGUAL LANGUAGE DEVELOPMENT

We have already seen that there is not a neat distinction between children bilingual from birth and those who become bilingual after the age of three or four, but, for now, let us think about children who are exposed to two languages from birth to consider what bilingual development looks like. In some respects, of course, they resemble monolingual children – we know that bilingual children go through the same sort of stages as monolingual children. Like monolingual children, they go through the stages of babbling, one-word and two-word utterances at much the same time, although they may not do this at exactly the same time in both languages (Yip, 2013: 119). However, their situation is indeed different from that of monolingual children, as there are two different languages in the input. But do *they* know that? Early research suggested that children start out with a single system, containing words from both languages. We saw above that early researchers such as Ronjat (1913) and Leopold (1949) stressed the importance of keeping the input of the two languages separate. Although Leopold (1949) had already suggested that mixing of the two languages by the child was evidence that they started out with a single underlying system, a later influential publication in the field was Volterra and Taeschner's (1978) article about two German-Italian-learning children, which very much supported Leopold's position. Research since then, however, has challenged this view and the current majority consensus is that bilingual children who are regularly exposed to two languages develop them as independent systems (Serratrice, 2013: 87). Serratrice, however, goes on to point out that this does not mean that the two languages are completely autonomous, noting that the current focus of much research is the interaction between the two languages. We will consider this cross-linguistic issue shortly. First, let us consider how very young children can tell the languages apart. As we saw in Chapter 3, we know from research into monolingual infants that they have sophisticated perceptual abilities from an early age (Jusczck, 1997; DeCasper and Fifer, 1980; Mehler *et al.*, 1988). De Houwer (2009: 157) notes that it is the melodic aspects of speech, the intonation contours, that are detectable by babies in the womb and that new-borns are sensitive to prosodic aspects of speech (pitch, rhythm and stress). In the case of infants raised in a bilingual environment, it appears that they are indeed sensitive to both languages. In an important study, Byers-Heinlein *et al.* (2010) tested new-borns within five days of birth and demonstrated that the bilingual babies who had heard Tagalog and English when in the womb showed no preference for either language, whereas the babies who had heard only English preferred this, showing at the same time that they were able to tell the languages apart. This was possibly aided by the fact that the two languages are rhythmically different. However, as we saw in Chapter 3, Bosch and Sebastián-Gallés's (2001) Spanish-Catalan subjects were able to detect differences between the two languages below five months of age, despite prosodic similarities between the languages.

However, the process of distinguishing the phonemes of language is later than the melodic aspects. We saw in Chapter 2 what the monolingual baby has to do in terms of speech perception – now we need to think about the bilingual baby's task in learning to discriminate two sets of phonemes. Bilingual babies do indeed learn to distinguish sound contrasts that are relevant to the languages they are acquiring by the middle of their second year (de Houwer, 2009: 163). Sundara *et al.* (2008) tested English–French bilinguals and French and English monolinguals at six to eight months and the bilingual babies were able to tell the difference between the French dental and the English alveolar pronunciation of /d/. Currently, then, the evidence suggests that in terms of speech perception bilingual babies do not lag behind monolingual ones. However, it is worth bearing in mind that it can be difficult to make comparisons as there may be an effect of the particular pair of languages being learned as some pairs may be more similar to – or different from – others (Serratrice, 2013: 90).

Given that the evidence points to infants being aware of their speech environment, we need next to look at what they actually produce. We saw in Chapter 3 that babies go through quite a long period of babbling, starting at three months and progressively containing consonants and vowels, in addition to yells, squeals, raspberries and so on. Around eight to nine months, children produce vowel–consonant combinations, a stage known as canonical babbling. It is generally thought that babies' early vocalisations are not language-specific, but that they gradually approximate to the language they are hearing towards the end of the first year. As they do, they strengthen their ability to discriminate these sounds while their ability to perceive sound contrasts that are not applicable to their language gradually declines (see Saxton, 2017: 126). So how do bilingual babies behave? As even with monolingual children researchers stress the variation that exists, it is difficult to pinpoint whether bilingual babies are really any different. A few studies suggest that the babbling reflects the two languages. For example, Poulin-Dubois and Goodz (2001) found support, albeit tentative, for early differentiation in the babbling of their French–English bilingual subjects aged ten to thirteen months, who appeared to use different consonants when speaking with French- or English-speaking parents. Anecdotally, when our daughter was placed in a French-speaking environment for a holiday at the age of fifteen months, we observed a change in her babbling to include more French-sounding vowels.

Like monolingual children, bilingual children produce **first words** around the end of the first year. The words in their vocabulary reflect the input they receive, as you would expect. Depending on the precise family situation, they may have what are called 'translation equivalents' – that is, they know the word for something in both languages. It is highly likely that everyday words for food, toys and regular activities will have **translation equivalents**. Parents often 'coach' the child by saying something like, 'what does daddy call this?' Conversely, there may be things that are known in only one language, if, for example, one parent always undertakes a particular activity, like going swimming. It is difficult to make generalisations about bilingual children's vocabularies, given the variety of possible contexts. However, some research has focused on the size of the **lexicon** in bilingual acquisition, and the relationship between this and the input. Teachers and parents are sometimes concerned that bilingual children may be lacking in vocabulary and the potential implications for their educational progress this may have. In this regard, it is worth making a distinction between comprehension and production.

Like monolingual children, comprehension generally precedes production (de Houwer, 2009: 210), so that children may understand many more words than they can say, as was the case with Manuela, Deuchar and Quay's subject (2000: 55). As noted already, they may not always have translation equivalents, but when they do it can be a case of comprehending both but producing only one of them – or pronouncing one more accurately in one language than the other. This may be because the opportunity to talk about something does not arise so often in one of the languages or because the pronunciation in one language is more difficult; as we saw in Chapter 3, some sounds are harder to produce than others and may be later acquired. So if, for example, a word in one language starts with a plosive like /t/ but the translation equivalent starts with a sound later acquired it may be avoided or inaccurately rendered. Similarly, consonant clusters (e.g. the 'str' in 'straw') may prove tricky. And, of course, the word in one language may be one syllable and in the other multisyllabic.

Not surprisingly, the **rate** at which bilingual children grow their vocabulary varies hugely, as is the case with monolingual children. Some children have a steady growth in vocabulary while others start off producing little but then experience a 'vocabulary spurt'. In the case of bilingual children, this spurt may not affect both languages equally. This may be occasioned by circumstance, such as a trip to visit grandparents who only speak one of the languages, or finding a playmate who shares the language. Even allowing for such variation, however, de Houwer (2009: 227) points out that if the two languages grow at different rates, this does not mean there is no relationship between the two, as it seems that children who are 'good talkers' in one language are the same in the other language, tending overall to make similar rates of progress in both. In terms of the overall size of the lexicon, that is, the number of words produced by bilingual children, de Houwer concludes on the basis of a number of studies that bilingual children do not produce fewer words in each language than monolingual children, arguing that this 'shows that contrary to what is often claimed, a "bilingual" setting is not a danger to the acquisition process' (2009: 229). However, Serratrice (2013: 95) reports that, in terms of receptive vocabulary, studies show that bilingual children tend to have smaller receptive vocabularies than age-matched monolingual children. She goes on to suggest that a more useful way of considering lexical knowledge in bilinguals is to think in terms of total conceptual vocabulary – that is, when one pools words from both languages, the total coverage is similar regardless of language background and possibly larger for bilinguals (2013: 96).

So far, we have seen that bilingual children fare pretty well with the sound system and the acquisition of vocabulary in their two languages. What happens with the grammar, however?

We saw in Chapter 3 that monolingual children start to combine words around eighteen months to two years of age and that there is considerable variation with this. Bilingual children show the same variation but are not delayed in comparison to monolingual children, as they too combine words from around the same age. Some children combine words in each of their two languages, some start combining in one language before the other and some produce combinations of the two languages. It is generally thought (see Chapter 3) that monolingual children need a lexicon of about 50 words before they begin combining them and this appears also to be the case with bilingual children. At this early stage and even as children move into combining three or more words, their utterances are still un-adult-like, as they lack closed class items and bound (grammatical) morphemes. Again, bilingual children follow this pattern. Generally speaking, as they develop, the utterances produced in each language tend to mimic the language the children hear. This means that, overall, each language tends to follow the path of monolingual usage (de Houwer, 2009: 290). For example, Meisel (1989, 2001) noted that the French–German bilingual children in his study produced different word order sequences in both languages as soon as they began to produce multi-word utterances. However, the increase in grammatical complexity is also related in part to utterance *length* in that children who produce longer utterances also produce more grammatically complex ones. Furthermore, for both monolingual and bilingual children, there appears to be a strong relationship between the size of the lexicon and subsequent grammatical development. In a study of 113 Spanish–English bilingual children, Marchman *et al.* (2004) found that there was a strong association between vocabulary and grammar *within* each language. In other words, grammatical skills in English were predicted by English vocabulary and grammatical skills in Spanish were predicted by Spanish vocabulary.

This brings us back to the issue of how separate the two languages are – Serratrice (2013: 97) points out that Marchman *et al.*'s findings are in line with the hypothesis that simultaneous bilinguals treat their two languages as largely independent systems. This does not mean that there is no interaction between the two languages, and **cross-linguistic influence** has been suggested by a number of studies over the last twenty years or so. Cross-linguistic influence may mean that one language is in some way affected by the other – Hulk (2000) noted the effect of Dutch word order on the French of their bilingual child, Anouk, for example. However, de Houwer (2009: 296) argues that the evidence is slim, particularly in children under the age of four. The interaction between the two languages is perhaps most noticeable when children produce **mixed utterances**, something that has long been observed. As Genesee (1989: 161) commented, 'virtually all studies of infant bilingual development have found that bilingual children mix elements from their two languages'. Clearly at the single word stage, they are unable to produce mixed utterances, although word blends may appear. For instance, Adèle's word for 'leaf' was 'leuf', a mix of the English 'leaf' and the French 'feuille'. Of course, while observers may *notice* these mixed utterances, this may be simply because the hearer just doesn't understand the other language. In all likelihood, utterances account for only a small minority of what children produce, particularly as they get older. This is also something that can change over time (de Houwer, 2009). As the child's lexicon grows, there are probably more transition equivalents and the 'right' word is available in the 'right' language, or possibly as pronunciation develops, a word that was previously difficult to say becomes more accessible. Equally, as children mature, they begin to recognise that not all the people they speak to will understand both languages. Once children combine words, however, what do they mix? De Houwer (2009: 292) suggests that a key characteristic is that in most cases the child inserts a single word from one language into the other, and the word is most likely to be a noun. Pettito *et al.* (2001) noted that the greatest occurrence of 'guest' words comprised nouns or other content words, introduced into the host language, typically the language of the addressee (2001: 32), suggesting a systematic and non-random approach to mixing that relies on the children's interlocutor sensitivity, as in the example above where Adèle translated into French for me! This pragmatic choice may be one reason children mix, but others have suggested that it may be related to the input.

For example, Goodz (1989) found that even with parents who claimed to adhere to the one person – one language strategy, language mixing by parents and children was closely related and parents tended to respond to children's mixed utterances with mixed utterances of their own (1989: 38). Pettito *et al.* (2001: 28) also found that the rate of mixing in the children's language in their study was directly related to their parents' rate of language mixing. In Byers-Heinlein's (2013) study, most parents reported regular language mixing in interactions with their child. Does this matter?

De Houwer (2007), in a large-scale survey of 1,899 families where one parent spoke the majority language and the other spoke a minority language, emphasises strongly the importance of the pattern of parental input. She suggests that parents who might have decided to each use both languages might be well advised to restrict the use of the majority language so that only one of them uses it, and notes that whereas raising children to speak a single language has a 100 per cent success rate (except in some cases of impairment), raising children to speak two languages only has a 75 per cent success rate (2007: 421–2). Earlier in this chapter we mentioned Grosjean's concept of 'wax and wane'. Yet if one of a child's two languages is heard and used less frequently and, in addition, is not the language of the community, on arrival at nursery or school, there is a risk there is only 'wane'. Indeed, we have seen the range of different situations in which bilingual children grow up and it is easy to see how this can lead to uneven development in the two languages. As the best outcome for the child is fluency and competence in both the languages, teachers and cargivers need to ask themselves how best to support early bilingualism (or plurilingualism), particularly when there is limited or little exposure to the minority language. Practical suggestions include information-finding: bearing in mind the range of possible contexts, it is very useful to know which languages the child speaks with whom and how often, whether they have exposure to books, television and so on in which languages. Children can be encouraged to bring books into school to share and display, to add to any bilingual books ordered by the school. We know how important it is for children to use their languages, so we can ask children to use their other language(s) wherever possible and to share and teach other children and to work together if possible with other speakers of that language. As children get older, as we saw in Chapter 4, they become able to talk about their languages as metalinguistic awareness develops. De Houwer (2009: 324) stresses the importance of the **attitudes** that school and peers have towards the languages involved and to child bilingualism in general. For example, Kirsch and Aleksic (2018), in the context of Luxembourg, found that a fifteen-hour-long course for pre-school teachers resulted in a significant increase in the promotion of the children's home languages, particularly in planned activities such as singing, rhyming and storytelling. They also began to understand that the use of their home language(s) was not the impediment that they had believed it to be. The importance of partnerships between practitioners and parents/families cannot be underestimated. For example, a project investigating parental views in a multilingual pre-school in Sweden increased the early years' practitioners' awareness of the need to incorporate the children's wider linguistic repertoire (Axelsson, 2008: 89).

CHAPTER SUMMARY

In this chapter, we have seen how bilingualism or plurilingualism is the norm around the world, and that it is very natural for speakers to draw upon their full linguistic repertoire. We made a distinction between simultaneous and consecutive bilingualism, although this is not always clear-cut. Nevertheless, in considering simultaneous bilingualism, we can see that growing up with more than one language is in no way disadvantageous – on the contrary, this is something to welcome and nurture. Far from being confused, young children are adept at understanding and using both languages and, while there may be some mixed utterances, this is nothing to be concerned about. Bilingual children largely share the same milestones as monolingual children, which suggests that concern about delay is misplaced. However, this does not mean that both languages always develop to the same degree, as we know that the contexts of bilingual development can vary enormously, so that the vital opportunities for input and interaction (see Chapter 1) vary in turn. And while we may think of bilingualism as a family affair, in fact teachers and caregivers have a crucial role to play.

REFERENCES

Axelsson, M. (2008) Multilingual pre-schools in Sweden: finding out what parents really want. In C. Kenner and T. Hickey (eds), *Multilingual Europe: Diversity and Learning*. Stoke-on-Trent: Trentham, 84–8.

Barron-Hauwert, S. (2011) *Bilingual Siblings: Language Use in Families*. Bristol: Multilingual Matters

Bosch, L. and Sebastián-Gallés, N. (2001) Early language differentiation in bilingual infants. In J. Cenoz and F. Genesee (eds), *Trends in Bilingual Acquisition Research*. Amsterdam: John Benjamins.

Byers-Heinlein, K. (2013) Parental language mixing: its measurement and the relation of mixed input to young bilingual children's vocabulary size. *Bilingualism: Language and Cognition*, 16(1), 32–48.

Byers-Heinlein, K., Burns, T.C. and Werker, J.F. (2010) The roots of bilingualism in newborns. *Psychological Science*, 21(3), 343–8.

Conteh, J. (2007) Culture, languages and learning: mediating a bilingual approach in complementary Saturday classes. In J. Conteh, P. Martin and L. Helavaara Robertson (eds), *Multilingual Learning: Stories from Schools and Communities in Britain*. Stoke-on-Trent: Trentham, 119–34.

Coulmas, F. (2018) *An Introduction to Multilingualism: Language in a Changing World*. Oxford: Oxford University Press.

Crystal, D. (2004) *The Language Revolution*. Cambridge: Polity Press.

de Houwer, A. (1995) Bilingual language acquisition. In P. Fletcher and B. MacWhinney (eds), *The Handbook of Child Language*. Oxford: Oxford University Press.

de Houwer, A. (2007) Parental language input patterns and children's bilingual use. *Applied Psycholinguistics*, 28, 411–24.

de Houwer, A. (2009) *Bilingual First Language Acquisition*. Bristol: Multilingual Matters.

DeCasper, A.J. and Fifer, W.P. (1980) Of human bonding: newborns prefer their mothers' voices. *Science*, 208, 1174–6.

Deuchar, M. and Quay, S. (2000) *Bilingual Acquisition: Theoretical Implications of a Case Study*. Oxford: Oxford University Press.

Ethnologue (ongoing) https://www.ethnologue.com/ (accessed 7 September 2011).

Genesee, F. (1989) Early bilingual development: one language or two? *Journal of Child Language*, 16, 161–79.

Goodz, N.S. (1989) Parental language mixing in bilingual families. *Infant Mental Health Journal*, 10(1), 25–44.

Grosjean, F. (2013) Bilingualism: a short introduction. In F. Grosjean and P. Li (eds), *The Psycholinguistics of Bilingualism*. Hoboken, NJ: John Wiley & Sons, 5–25.

Heller, M. (ed.) (2007) *Bilingualism: A Social Approach*. Hampshire: Palgrave Macmillan.

Hoffmann, C. (1991) *An Introduction to Bilingualism*. London: Longman.

Hulk, A. (2000) Non-selective access and activation in child bilingualism: the syntax. In S. Döpke (ed.), *Cross-Linguistic Structures in Simultaneous Bilingualism*. Amsterdam: John Benjamins.

Juszczk, P.W. (1997) *The Discovery of Spoken Language*. Cambridge, MA: MIT Press.

Kenner, C. and Ruby, M. (2012) *Interconnecting Worlds: Teacher Partnerships for Bilingual Learning*. Stoke-on-Trent: Trentham.

Kenner, C., Gregory, E., Jessel, J., Ruby, M. and Arju, T. (2004) Intergenerational learning between children and grandparents in east London. Project Report. ESRC, Swindon: Goldsmiths Research. Available at: http://eprints.gold.ac.uk/4533/ (accessed 21 October 2019).

Kirsch, C. and Aleksic, G. (2018) The effect of professional development on multilingual education in early childhood in Luxembourg. *Review of European Studies*, 10(4), 148–63.

Lenneberg, E. (1967) *The Biological Foundations of Language*. New York: Wiley.

Leopold, W.F. (1949/1970) *Speech Development of a Bilingual Child: A Linguist's Record. Vol III Grammar and General Problems in the First Two Years*. New York: AMS Press.

Macrory, G. (2006) Bilingual language development: what do early years practitioners need to know? *Early Years: An International Journal of Research and Development*, 26(2), 159–70.

Marchman, V.A., Martínez-Sussmann, C. and Dale, P.S. (2004) The language-specific nature of grammatical development: evidence from bilingual language learners. *Developmental Science*, 7(2), 212–24.

McLaughlin, B. (1984) *Second Language Acquisition in Childhood. Vol I: The Preschool Years*. 2nd edn. Hove: Lawrence Erlbaum.

Mehler, J., Jusczyk, P.W., Lambertz, G., Halsted, N., Bertoncini, J. and Amiel-Tison, C. (1988) A precursor of language acquisition in young infants. *Cognition*, 29, 143–78.

Meisel, J. (1989) Early differentiation of languages in bilingual children. In K. Hyltenstam and L. Obler (eds), *Bilingualism Across the Lifespan: Aspects of Acquisition, Maturity and Loss*. Cambridge: Cambridge University Press.

Meisel, J. (2001) The simultaneous acquisition of two languages: early differentiation and subsequent development of grammars. In J. Cenoz and F. Genesee (eds), *Trends in Bilingual Acquisition Research*. Amsterdam: John Benjamins.

Meisel, J.M. (2008) Child second language acquisition or successive first language acquisition? In B. Haznedar and E. Gavruseva (eds), *Current Trends in Child Second Language Acquisition*. Amsterdam: Benjamins, 55–80.

Panayi, P. (2020) *Migrant City: A New History of London*. New Haven: Yale University Press.

Pettito, L.A., Katerelos, M., Levy, B., Gauna, G., Tétreault, K. and Ferraro, V. (2001) Bilingual signed and spoken language acquisition from birth: implications for the mechanisms underlying early bilingual acquisition. *Journal of Child Language*, 28, 453–96.

Poulin-Dubois, D. and Goodz, N. (2001) Language differentiation in bilingual infants: evidence from babbling. In J. Cenoz and F. Genesee (eds), *Trends in Bilingual Acquisition Research*. Amsterdam: John Benjamins.

Romaine, S. (1995) *Bilingualism*. 2nd edn. Oxford: Blackwell.

Ronjat, J. (1913) *Le développement du langage observe chez un enfant bilingue*. Paris: Champion.

Saunders, G. (1988) *Bilingual Children: From Birth to Teens*. Bristol: Multilingual Matters.

Saxton, M. (2017) *Child Language*. 2nd edn. London: SAGE.

Serratrice, L. (2013) The bilingual child. In T.K. Bhatia and W.C. Ritchie, *The Handbook of Bilingualism and Multilingualism*. 2nd edn. Oxford: Wiley-Blackwell.

Sundara, M., Polka, L. and Molnar, M. (2008) Development of coronal stop perception: bilingual infants keep pace with their monolingual peers. *Cognition*, 108(1), 232–42.

Unsworth, S. and Hulk, A. (2009) Early successive bilingualism: disentangling the relevant factors. *Zeitschrift für Sprachwissenschaft*, 28, 69–77. doi 10.1515/ZFSW.2009.008

Volterra, V. and Taeschner, T. (1978) The acquisition and development of language by bilingual children. *Journal of Child Language*, 5, 311–26.

Yip, V. (2013) Simultaneous language acquisition. In F. Grosjean and P. Li (eds), *The Psycholinguistics of Bilingualism*. Hoboken, NJ: John Wiley & Sons, 119–44.

6

THE BILINGUAL CHILD: CONSECUTIVE BILINGUALISM

INTRODUCTION

In the last chapter, we saw how prevalent the use of more than one language is around the world and considered in particular the case of simultaneous bilingualism – that is, when children develop two languages from birth. In this chapter, we will look at consecutive – or successive – bilingualism, when children acquire their new language after the age of three or thereabouts. While, as we saw in Chapter 5, there are children who do not fall neatly into one of these categories, known as 'early successive' bilinguals (Unsworth and Hulk, 2009), here we will primarily focus on children who are acquiring a new language after three and typically upon arrival in nursery or school, or at any time – during the primary school years in a UK context, this can mean between the ages of three and eleven. Migration around the world makes this a common scenario and it is by no means a new phenomenon. Given the considerable changes brought about world-wide by globalisation, moving populations, changing political landscapes and the rapid

development of technology in the last twenty to 30 years, it is hardly surprising that there has been an upsurge of research into multilingualism (see
Martin-Jones *et al.*, 2012). The European Commission and the Council of
Europe point to the diversity of schools and classrooms, noting that the
school system should meet the needs of those from a wide variety of back-
grounds (European Commission, 2008; Council of Europe, 2018). As we
saw in Chapter 5, there are more than 300 languages spoken in London
alone (Panayi, 2020), and the percentage of children for whom English is
not their first language has risen greatly, such that Mistry and Sood (2020)
estimate that a fifth of the child population in England speaks a language
other than English at home. Beyond Europe, of course, there is a plurilingual tradition in many parts of the world, such as South Asia (Canagarajah,
2009), Africa (Dyers, 2013) and Latin America (Hamel, 2013). Other countries that we might associate with English such as Australia and North
America are also by no means exclusively English-speaking. The latter was
reported in 2015 by the American Census Bureau as having 350 languages,
while Australia also has more than 300 (Panayiotou *et al.*, 2019).

So, we can see that the UK is not out of step with the rest of the world.
In many places children are arriving at school not yet having acquired the
language of schooling, even though they may be bi- or plurilingual already
in other languages. In the UK, of course, the language of schooling is generally English and this chapter will try to address how best to support the
development of this in the school context. However, it is imperative to
stress that this must happen alongside the development of other languages
that children speak. The notion of 'English as an additional language' tends
to shift the focus on to English, and the frequently used acronym EAL can
serve to pigeon-hole children as having only this as their identity, which is
actually much more bound up with the other language(s) and culture(s)
that they live in. It therefore behoves us as practitioners not just to acknowledge, but to support and develop children's bilingualism or plurilingualism.
Part of this chapter will try to address this. We will also consider the important part that classroom foreign-language learning plays in developing a
bilingual population.

We will look at what it means to develop bilingualism consecutively as
opposed to simultaneously. While this chapter has a focus on learning the
language of schooling, we also need to consider the way in which taught
foreign languages contribute to the potential for creating a multilingual
world. With these scenarios in mind, we will first look at the possible difference that **age** of acquiring a new language makes, as well as what kind
of attainment we are looking for, particularly in the case of children acquiring the language of schooling. The kind of language (in the case of the UK,
English) that children need to learn in order to be successful in the school
system is very much related to what enables children to be successful in
exam terms, including the need to become literate. We addressed some

elements of this in Chapter 4. With the case of successive bilingualism still in mind, we will look at the developmental *path* that the learner takes – what do the early stages of language learning look like and what happens later? Then we will consider the second context for becoming bilingual: classroom foreign-language learning. The influence exerted by children's first language(s) in either scenario will be considered, along with factors that may affect the *rate* of progress that individual learners make. First of all, let us consider the question of age.

WHAT DIFFERENCE DOES AGE MAKE?

We noted in Chapter 1 and again in Chapter 5 that Lenneberg (1967) proposed a 'critical period' for language acquisition, which led to the CPH (critical period hypothesis) and which suggested that there was a finite period when a first language could be acquired. His proposal has generated a substantial amount of research and contemporary researchers are still unable to agree entirely about this. So how much truth is there in this idea and what are the implications for consecutive bilinguals? Let's recall what exactly Lenneberg proposed: namely, that there is a window that opens (the 'onset') at around two years of age, with the 'offset' around twelve, coinciding with puberty. Lenneberg was partly motivated by the Chomskyan notion of an innate language acquisition device (i.e. signalling that there may be a biological basis to language acquisition), and there appeared to be some evidence from other species that there were critical periods for development (Penfield and Roberts, 1959). Studies of feral or severely neglected children (see Curtiss *et al.*, 1974) also pointed to the difficulty of developing language after a certain age. However, many have noted the difficulties of disassociating the child's background and subsequent development. In reviewing evidence from neurological studies, feral children, deaf babies and children with Down's syndrome, Singleton and Ryan (2004) note that the evidence points to a much earlier sensitivity to acquire language than two years of age (as we saw in Chapter 3) and also point to considerable evidence that language competence develops well beyond the school years (as indeed we saw in Chapter 4). They conclude that there are no clear grounds for suggesting that language acquisition cannot occur after puberty (2004: 60).

However, we need to remember that there are many other variables that interact with the age of the learner and contribute to language learning outcomes (Murphy, 2015: 5). So, does this mean that it is difficult to become bilingual successively? Clearly not, although the age issue is one that influences policy decisions, such as the relatively recent introduction of taught foreign languages in primary school in England from the age of seven (September 2014). There is also a commonly heard view that young children 'pick up' languages easily and that they are like 'sponges'. We will explore this in more detail below. Although this notion is prevalent, there is in fact research that points to the superiority of adolescents and young adults in learning a new language (Snow and Hoefnagel-Höhle, 1978). This was in terms of **rate**. While, at the time, this appeared to contradict the view that there was a critical period for language learning, a rider to these findings came not long after, when some studies showed that over time, younger learners actually did better (see Long, 1990). They effectively overtook the older learners. Contemporary researchers tend to take a long-term view on ultimate attainment (Ortega, 2009: 17). However, it remains unclear exactly what effect age of arrival in the target language culture has. An oft-quoted study by Johnson and Newport (1989) showed positive effects of earlier arrival, but when this was replicated a few years later (Birdsong and Molis, 2001) the initial findings were not confirmed. Perhaps importantly, the researchers found that grammaticality judgements were related to the *amount* of current L2 usage. This is a further reminder that factors other than age are at play. Murphy (2015) suggests that it is not always helpful to compare bilinguals with monolingual speakers of the same language. Some studies have also found that there are individuals that start learning a new language much later than puberty who have very good attainment. This prompted Ortega (2009: 20) to conclude that doubts about a critical period for language learning are not going to go away while research results show that for some people there is no sharp drop in grammaticality intuitions after a certain age and while we still discover cases of exceptionally successful late learners. However, where researchers tend to agree is in the case of phonology (see Singleton and Ryan, 2004). A foreign accent is usually much more likely to mark the speech of an older learner than a younger one and, of course, in the case of pronunciation there are physical factors at play. While there are cases of older learners who develop a pronunciation very close to a native-speaker's, in general younger learners do better. This is also perhaps one of the reasons that young children appear to 'pick up' languages easily: they *sound* right. This is something we will return to below. However, before we do, it is perhaps worth noting that many of the studies that purport to show advantages for younger learners are undertaken in naturalistic contexts (Singleton and Ryan, 2004: 68). These, of course, offer more opportunities for input and interaction than formal learning environments.

The issue of ultimate attainment is important in terms of policy decisions – Ortega says that:

> knowing that young children may have a slow start when acquiring an L2 can be an important research-based argument against harmful attempts to promote so-called sink-or-swim educational policies that attempt to reduce or

even withdraw the first and second language support that is to be provided to language minority children by schools.

(Ortega, 2009: 28)

Recognition that young children need time is vital, as is an understanding of the different contexts for second-language learning. Murphy (2015: 5) stresses that although age may indeed be associated with language learning outcomes, we need to place it in the context of other variables. She points to the necessity of understanding age as a variable as fully as possible – without this understanding, she suggests, it might be assumed that if a child is exposed to the new language at an early age (before the end of any sensitive period), it might be expected that the child will acquire the new language without difficulty. Policy-makers may then assume that children simply need to be exposed to the new language when young, and will not need support for their learning. Murphy's 2015 book helpfully outlines different contexts for L2 learning, reminding us of the complexity of language learning and the role of the input. We may want to note, from a theoretical perspective, that (as we saw in Chapter 1) the notion of a biological basis to language and the CPH sits alongside the Chomskyan perspective that there is an innate predisposition to learn language (the language acquisition device). We have to counterbalance this with the view that input and context are crucially important. This further demonstrates the potential influence that different theoretical perspectives can have upon policy decisions.

WHAT IS THE END GOAL?

We noted above that we are focusing upon successive bilingualism in an educational setting, and that one aim is for children to be successful in the school system. Of course, the key aim is for children to grow up as confident, secure bilingual or plurilingual individuals who enjoy their cultures and are comfortable with their bilingual or plurilingual identity. Nevertheless, their future as adults depends very much upon educational success. I suggested above that we need to consider the *kind* of language that children need to learn. The work of Cummins (1979, 1980) is highly relevant in this regard and has been hugely influential. Essentially, he distinguishes between basic interpersonal communication skills (BICS) and cognitive academic language proficiency (CALP). The former, on the one hand, is what children develop quite quickly through interacting with adults and with their peers – the informal, everyday language (vocabulary and grammar) that characterises social communication and may contain predictable formulae. The latter, on the other hand, is the kind of language that is much more formal and, of course, highly characteristic of the education system – and the kind of language you need to understand and use in order to pass exams (see Nippold, 2016): CALP, then, is largely, though not exclusively, the written language of schooling. This is the kind of language we noted in Chapter 4 as being important for all children to develop as they go through the school years, although clearly children who arrive in the school system later than others will have a steeper learning curve and will continue to need support. Cummins suggested that children develop BICS first and CALP later, the former taking about two years and the latter between seven and ten years. This can be a useful distinction, but there are several things to bear in mind.

First, this is not to propose a linear model with one coming after the other. There is likely to be a degree of overlap as, even in the early stages of learning a new language, some more formal aspects are likely to be introduced into the classroom by the teacher. The age of the child is of relevance here too – a very young child will in all likelihood be using more BICS and less CALP, whereas an older child will be more quickly exposed to CALP in the classroom and may be picking up the more social language at the same time. Equally, an older child will have more metalinguistic awareness than a younger one and will be able to bring this to bear on the task of learning a new language, such as asking the meaning of words, memorising new words and so on. Other factors include the child's previous educational experience, as well as such things as personality and affective factors. So while it is helpful to be aware of the particular nature of the language needed for school success, it is not a clear-cut distinction. Of course, a younger child will have much longer to develop the academic skills needed and in that sense is more like a first-language speaker. A further issue is that, as we noted earlier, children tend to adopt a new phonological system more readily than adults, such that they often do not sound 'foreign' – this can make it easy to think they have just picked the language up and do not require support for the educational aspects. Cummins (1984) further elaborated the BICS/CALP theory by proposing a framework for language proficiency in which there are two continua: one continuum is the extent to which the communication is 'context-embedded' or 'context-reduced'; the other is the extent to which it is 'cognitively demanding' or 'cognitively undemanding'. He explicitly acknowledges the debt that this framework owes to Donaldson's (1978) distinction between embedded and disembedded thought and language. To elaborate a little more, let us think about what 'context-embedded' or 'context-reduced' actually means. Some activities contain many contextual clues as to what is going on, which, as we saw in the first chapter, is highly enabling to young children learning a first language. For instance, the routine of bath time with familiar toys, predictable sequence of events and language 'tied' to this is facilitative for language learning. Similarly, in a classroom situation, the setting up of a familiar and possibly repeated activity can aid the acquisition of language. In the case of very young children, this could involve, for example, role-play activity in a play house, sand and water play and so on. For older children, the setting up of a science activity, an art lesson or a sports lesson may provide valuable clues as to what the language means. In comparison, a set of spoken instructions with no context or a text or poem read aloud in class offer little (if anything) by way of clues. When we combine this with the idea of how cognitively challenging a task is, we have a useful tool to analyse classroom/school activities. The framework is known as the 'Cummins grid' or the 'Cummins matrix' (see Figure 6.1).

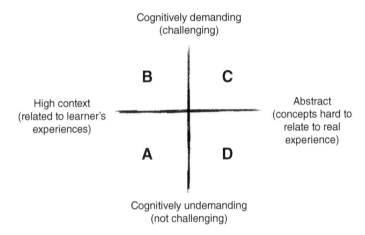

Figure 6.1 The Cummins grid

Using this matrix, teachers can assess which of the quadrants (A, B, C or D) the classroom activity falls in. Looking at the matrix, you can see that quadrant 'A' (bottom left) would be where you would place a task that is 'cognitively undemanding' and significantly related to the learner's own experiences. The opposite of this would be an activity in quadrant 'C' (diagonally opposite to quadrant 'A' in the diagram). To be placed here, an activity would be 'cognitively demanding' and abstract. 'Abstract' is defined in the diagram as 'concepts hard to relate to real experience'. Considering an activity's placements in this grid will help you to know how challenging it may be for children.

To illustrate this, what would an activity look like if it were both cognitively unchallenging *and* context-embedded? This could be simple face-to-face conversation, whereas a cognitively unchallenging and context-reduced task might be a list of simple instructions. The context-embedded but cognitively challenging example might be a science lesson with a demonstration. Finally, what might something both cognitively challenging *and* context-reduced be? Something like sitting down to an exam paper or turning on the radio without knowing in advance what you are going to hear might illustrate this. Of course, at times, perhaps to settle a child in, something that is unchallenging and context-embedded can be helpful. Learners, however, do have to progress towards handling the language needed in context-reduced, cognitively challenging situations if they are to be successful in the educational system. But the provision of context in the early stages (or at the beginning of a new topic) can easily be provided through visuals, diagrams and demonstrations. This is similar to Vygotsky's idea of scaffolding (see Chapter 1); with careful planning the scaffolding can be gradually dismantled until the learner can manage without it.

Two further important ideas promoted by Cummins are that of the Linguistic Interdependence Principle and the 'Common Underlying Proficiency Framework' (CUP) (1981, 2000). The notion of linguistic interdependence is that, with the right approach, both languages can be mutually supportive such that one language is not developed at the expense of the other. The CUP hypothesis is that focusing on the first language supports the development of the second – in other words, there is no detriment to focusing on the first language. Bilingual growth and the acquisition of the language of schooling are not in any way incompatible. This is important as if only one language is fully developed it is likely to be the language of schooling and we need to avoid loss of L1. And the younger the child on arrival at school the less well developed the L1 will be.

Having considered the 'end goal', we need to look at the process of language acquisition *towards* this goal.

BECOMING BILINGUAL: LEARNING A NEW LANGUAGE

Let us picture a common scenario. We will start with the younger child, say, three or four years old. She arrives in your class, possibly half way through the term and/or year, with no apparent English. The first thing to bear in mind is that this child is already a pretty accomplished talker – albeit in another language or languages. Even a child as young as this (or possibly younger) already knows quite a lot about language and communication. They can attend to the non-verbal aspects of communication (although these may vary culturally), are aware of the attitudes and emotions of others – they will understand that someone is happy, sad or cross. They know (unconsciously) that language can be used to *do* things: to request, complain, narrate, ask and answer questions and myriad other things. They know that they can use language to effect functions and that others can too. They know that language refers to things, people and events in the world. They know that speakers take turns and interact with each other. As for the form of language itself, they know, for example (again, unconsciously), that language is not random – words come in a certain order and they know that it is not only words but intonation that conveys meaning. So they are by no means a blank slate.

Faced with a new situation, possibly knowing no-one, children need time to absorb their surroundings and perhaps unsurprisingly many have been observed to go through a 'silent period' (Gibbons, 1985), although others have questioned how consistent and typical this is (e.g. Roberts, 2014). Apparent silence sometimes causes concern on the part of teachers, but is nothing to worry about and can last for some time. Some have suggested that during this period children are engaged in language learning strategies, such as private speech (Saville-Troike, 1988). What is important for teachers and caregivers is to observe the overall behaviour of the child – not just the language – and to understand how bilingual children behave beyond the classroom (Drury, 2013). Young children's behaviour in these early days and weeks can vary, of course. A child who has fled a war zone and witnessed distressing events is in a very different situation from the child whose arrival is part of a great adventure because a parent is here to undertake a higher degree. However, we should not assume that what appears to adults to be a positive reason for movement to another country is without difficulty for a young child, who may nevertheless be missing friends and grandparents, for example. This underlines the importance of finding out as much as possible about the child's background. And young children have different personalities – some will listen and observe, others will 'have a go' at the new language.

In the beginning stages of learning a new language, once children begin to produce utterances, their linguistic behaviour will probably parallel that of children learning the language as a first language. So they may start to notice and then produce single salient words or short multi-word utterances. Depending on how different the phonology of the first language is to the new language, the accuracy of pronunciation may vary, and children will need time and practice to get this right. Some sounds may be completely new (think 'th' for a French-speaking child), others similar but not quite the same; the *combination* of sounds may be different from the child's first language – the combination 'str' (as in straw) may be especially tricky as not all languages require a speaker to produce these in succession without a vowel in between – notably Japanese, which largely has syllables composed of one consonant and one vowel. As we saw in Chapter 2, languages are generally stress-timed or syllable-timed so there are clear implications for moving from one type to another, both in terms of listening and speaking. Understanding a new language, then, is tricky! Children will be trying to 'map' what they hear onto the world around them, which is why contextual support is very useful in the early days. From a grammatical perspective, these early utterances are likely to be formulaic, learned in context and associated with particular events or activities. As in monolingual first-language acquisition, lexical items may be subject to over- or underextension, although, of course, the older a child is, the more likely they are to be aware that they are not using the 'right' word. We will come back to the age issue shortly. They will gradually build up a larger repertoire of words and utterances. In so doing, however, like first-language users of the language, they will make errors. Many of these errors will resemble those made by monolingual children acquiring English as a first language from birth. So we should expect to see errors such as 'wented' and 'sheeps' in children developing bilingually. This is entirely to be expected as such errors reflect an underlying appreciation of pattern in language and the ability to make analogies. Returning briefly to the issue of age, we need to remember that the younger a child is the more they will resemble a first-language speaker. Conversely, the older a child is, the more noticeable such errors may be as they appear to be inconsistent with the child's age and cognitive maturity. And as we tend to associate such errors with a younger child, it is absolutely vital that we do not allow our perception of the child to be influenced by this in a negative way. Older children have more advanced metalinguistic awareness and may be well aware of the fact that their new language is not on a par with their first language(s). They may also be able to ask questions, understand explanations and rules and make comparisons with their other language(s). They therefore bring an advantage that younger children do not – which is potentially helpful given that the older they are at the point where they start to learn English, the steeper the incline they need to climb in order to 'catch up' with their first-language peers.

Children are not passive, so how do they go about this? One seminal study is that of Wong-Fillmore (1979), whose research focused in particular upon one of five immigrant children that she observed as they interacted and played with their English-speaking peers at a school in the US in the 1970s – a child called Nora, who was approaching six at the time. None of the children was receiving any formal English instruction during the period of the study. While Wong-Fillmore was of the view that there were going to be enormous differences between the five children, they nevertheless all seemed to share a number of social and cognitive strategies, admittedly with differing degrees of success. She summarised these as follows: social strategies included: S1) join a group and act as if you understand what is going on, even if you don't; S2) give the impression, with a few well-chosen words, that you speak the language; and S3) count on your friends for help. The cognitive strategies she noted were: C1) assume that what people are saying is relevant to the situation in hand; C2) get some expressions you understand and start talking; C3) look for recurring parts in the formulae you know; C4) make the most of what you've got; and C5) work on the big things first: save the details for later. What was important about this study was the focus on the role of formulae in language acquisition, not only in terms of the social function that these can perform but also in terms of the way in which they provide input that the child can analyse to seek out the patterns (see C3). This has clear parallels with more recent research that we looked at in Chapter 1, where we saw that the input was extremely important in acquisition. Not only this, but the more recent research paradigm associated with Tomasello and colleagues points to the sophisticated abilities of young children to discern abstract patterns from the input they receive and use. The other notable feature here is that we can see that children use language learning strategies – something that has attracted much research over the intervening years. Indeed, this has informed approaches to classroom teaching (see, for example, Grenfell and Harris, 2017; Chamot and Harris, 2019).

WHAT ABOUT THE LATER STAGES OF LANGUAGE LEARNING/LITERACY?

There are several things to consider here. We have already noted Cummins' suggestion that there is something he calls CALP, which refers to the academic language generally needed for school success, both spoken and written. However, before considering this in more detail, we should recall the features of later language we described in Chapters 3 and 4. For example, those tricky modal auxiliaries need to be acquired by the bilingual learner. Without these, as we saw, it is difficult to engage in spoken language that speculates, hypothesises and so on. It will take time to master such complexities, particularly if the first language handles these differently. And, of course, the later stages of oral language learning inevitably overlap with literacy. While this book is primarily concerned with learning to talk, it would be incomplete without some consideration of the place of **written language** in development (see Chapter 4). As we saw in that chapter, young children have to acquire the language of the written word – as the written word is not simply spoken language written down, particularly when it comes to the language of schooling.

What sort of challenge is this for young bilingual children? Much depends on what we might call their 'starting points':

a) previously literate in a Roman orthography (writing system) like English, e.g. a French-speaking child;
b) previously literate in another alphabetic writing system, e.g. Arabic;
c) previously literate in a non-alphabetic writing system, such as Mandarin;
d) not previously literate in any language.

This is not a simple case of (a) being the most straightforward and (d) the trickiest. On the one hand, while the French-speaking child may find the letters (graphemes) familiar, both to recognise and write, the different phoneme–grapheme correspondences have the potential to cause confusion. But the orthography also works in the same direction, from left to right and some of the punctuation will be familiar. In the case of (b), a child will have some understanding of the relationship between the phonemes and the graphemes, given that this is the principle of an alphabetic writing system. Other scripts that are alphabetic include Arabic, Hindi and Bengali. However, these may be written from right to left and may vary in which sounds the graphemes actually represent – in Arabic, for instance, not all vowels are represented in writing. Children who have been brought up with a non-alphabetic system (c) may not have the same appreciation of the relationship between sounds and letters. To those of us used to an alphabetic system, it may seem inconceivable that a writing system does not represent language at the level of the phoneme. There are, in fact, three kinds of writing system: in addition to the very common alphabetic one, we have syllabic and morphemic systems. An example of a syllabic system is the Japanese Katakana script, where each written symbol represents a syllable – as all syllables are composed of consonant–vowel (CV) combinations, it is unnecessary to have symbols for the individual phonemes. As readers, you are probably aware of the way the Mandarin writing system uses 'Chinese characters'. This is a morphemic system whereby the characters represent morphemes – that is, units of meaning. Although the left part of the character can contain clues to pronunciation, the character is essentially predicated upon meaning. Admittedly a somewhat simplistic comparison is with numbers: we can 'read' 2 + 2 = 4 as 'two and two make four' or 'deux et deux font quatre' – or in any language. But this does illustrate the fact that symbols on the page do not have to be related to sound. A comparison with English (oddly!) may also help here: although we tend to think of English as phonemic, an idea reinforced by recent emphases on phonics as the appropriate way to teach early reading, in fact it is not wholly phonemic – it is actually morpho-phonemic as it possesses characteristics that map onto meaning. Consider, for example, the past tense written ending <–ed>. When we see this we 'see' past tense, but in fact the word 'liked' actually ends in /t/. Similarly the plural <–s> represents the sound /z/ in 'dogs' and /s/ in 'cats'. Other lexical items retain the spelling of the base morpheme – so we retain the spelling of 'critic' in the word 'criticise' even though the letter <c> at the end of the morpheme <critic> is now pronounced /s/. This is an immense advantage to the skilled reader who can read by 'eye'. And in the case of (d), the extent to which this is a challenge is very dependent upon age: a three-year-old will be very similar to peers whereas a nine-year-old will not – but with increased cognitive skills and memory and the right support may quickly catch up.

BECOMING BILINGUAL: CLASSROOM FOREIGN-LANGUAGE LEARNING

Learning the language of schooling, however, is not the only route to bilingual competence. Young children in many countries in the world are offered the opportunity to become bilingual or plurilingual by learning another language as part of the primary school curriculum. In the UK, this has been a compulsory part of the curriculum since 2014, when all children aged seven and over are required to learn another language. In other countries, the starting age varies, so that, for example, in Europe, almost all countries now expect children to have begun learning a foreign language (FL) by the age of nine years, with many starting by seven years (Enever, 2011). The issues discussed earlier regarding the role of age in language learning have been highly pertinent to policy decisions surrounding curriculum planning, of course. Other theoretical considerations include the role of the input: as we have seen, the input and the opportunity to use language have enormous implications for language development. A crucial issue then in taught foreign-language contexts is the amount of curriculum time that can be devoted to it. Inevitably, there are differences in the experience of a child learning English in many other countries (where the use of English may be quite common) and a child learning French in a UK primary school. We have already mentioned the input available, and in the case of the latter this may be limited to just a couple of twenty-minute sessions a week. A prominent issue in the teaching of primary foreign languages is also the competence and confidence of the teacher, not just in terms of language competence but in appropriate pedagogy; while we cannot address this in detail here, it is nevertheless important to understand what 'learning to talk' means in this particular context. We have seen that young children have impressive language-learning capacities and the ability to draw upon their repertoire. In the same way as young children becoming bilingual through learning English in an English-speaking school system, those learning, say, Spanish, in a taught language classroom are able to make inferences, draw upon their first language(s) knowledge and adopt communicative strategies to convey meaning. They bring a wealth of knowledge to the experience and there is much for teachers to build upon.

WHAT ABOUT THE INFLUENCE OF THE FIRST LANGUAGE(S)?

In both the scenarios outlined above, children developing bilingually will of course make errors. First, we have seen that children developing bilingually in the school context will show some similarities to monolingual first-language speakers in the course of development and in the kinds of errors they produce. However, there are also differences – as we might expect. There will be some degree of cross-linguistic influence (as we saw with simultaneous bilingualism); it is perhaps inevitable and unsurprising that the first language will exert some influence. For example, if the rules for word order in the new language are different, it may need a certain amount of input (or in the case of an older child, an explanation) for the child to realise that something else is expected. So some errors can be explained by recourse to features of the first language (Swan and Smith,

2001). They may make errors based on the influence of their first language(s). For example, Urdu learners of English may find articles difficult as they are absent in Urdu, and English learners of German are likely to make errors with the case system as this does not exist in English. They may make hypotheses about the new language – as a child, knowing that the French for mustard was 'moutarde', I simply assumed the French for custard was 'coutarde'! And I was quite old before I realised my error to the extent that our family word for custard is 'coutarde' to this day. Children (and indeed adults) may also make errors based on an overextension of the patterns of the new language. This is as likely to happen in the foreign-language classroom situation as it is in the immersion situation of a child learning the language of schooling. Just as young learners of English may assume that the past tense ending is always '–ed', resulting in such errors as 'he goed', learners of French may overgeneralise endings on past participles, producing such items as 'jai prendu' instead of the irregular form 'j'ai pris'. Many of the children starting a taught foreign language in primary school will know a great deal about language through already being bilingual or plurilingual, and thus bring great advantage to the learning experience. For those that come to this experience as monolinguals, it offers them an invaluable opportunity to embark upon the path of becoming bilingual, like the majority of the world's population.

MAINTAINING AND ENHANCING FIRST LANGUAGE(S)

So, learning a new language is in no way 'out with the old and in with the new'! In fact, it is quite the contrary. We saw in Chapter 5 the importance of children developing *bilingually* and noted how vital it is for teachers and families to work together on this. In the case of successive bilingualism, perhaps all the more so when children are older on arrival in the English-dominant school system, it may seem tempting to prioritise the development of English in order to secure the best possible educational outcome for the child. However, there are other considerations here. For example, children's first language(s) are a **linguistic resource** that allows them to compare and contrast languages. Clearly this is a function of age, as older children have greater metalinguistic awareness. But opportunities to use the home languages in school can serve as a bridge between home and school, and particularly where there are other children who share the language, the chance to talk freely and without effort. The emotional aspects of learning a new language cannot be overstated – it is potentially tiring and frustrating. Furthermore, as Curdt-Christiansen and Huang note (2020: 177), children's home language(s) may have emotional connotations and deep personal meanings. They suggest that using the primary language can invoke deep emotional reactions and make family members feel 'closer' in daily interactions.

Thus the emotional well-being of children and their family members is of paramount importance. Yet those same family members may also be unsure how to proceed in this new context, and their decisions about language use – their 'family language policy' – may be affected by external factors such as the perceived status of different languages, the educational outcomes they desire for their children and, crucially, the attitudes of teachers and other professionals. Drury (2004: 51), writing about bilingual children in pre-school, suggests that children quickly learn that they need to prioritise English; she argues that teachers need to explicitly recognise first-language development if the children are not to lose their home languages. How can teachers do this? A recent project in Ireland with four- to five-year-olds (O'Rourke, 2011) introduced teachers to practical activities such as making a language flower with their home language at the centre, writing hello in a range of languages and integrating multilingual activities across the curriculum, such as making multilingual posters in science about the life cycle of the butterfly. Initially some staff expressed concern about how to manage the range of languages in their classes and the possible negative effect upon the learning of English, but in fact the project raised teachers' awareness of the range of languages spoken and they became more confident in dealing with situations where several languages were present in the classroom (O'Rourke, 2011: 120). The project also had an important effect upon parents, who could see from displays the work that the children had been doing. Also, teachers asked for support with such things as correct pronunciation, which led to conversations with the parents about their children's bilingualism. It then became possible to dispel misconceptions – for example, the project was able to change the perspective of a parent who had been advised by a nurse to speak English and not the home language, Romanian, at home. Projects such as these demonstrate in practical terms how bilingualism can be supported, be it simultaneous or successive.

FACTORS AFFECTING THE RATE OF PROGRESS IN THE NEW LANGUAGE

Turning back to the new language now, we have looked at some aspects of the route – the developmental path – that children may follow. Equally important, however, is their rate of progress. We alluded to this earlier when thinking about the possible silent period. As noted above, the reason for relocating may affect children's receptiveness to the new language, as may their personality. A shy and nervous child is different from an outgoing, risk-taking child. A child may feel self-conscious about their performance in the new language, be anxious about understanding what is going on or frustrated by their inability to show their 'real' self. This may in turn affect their motivation, as we cannot assume that motivation is a given. A lack of motivation may be linked to reasons for moving, but there are other considerations. Success or otherwise in a new language may influence one's motivation – on a positive note, the desire to make friends or do well academically may play a part. Equally, their particular family circumstances have a part to play. Where there are family members who already speak English, this is likely to be supportive of the child's progress, although this should not be at the expense of the home language.

In the primary foreign-language classroom there will also be variation in progress and outcomes. As noted already, major factors include the small amount of curriculum time and the confidence of the teacher. The limited exposure and practice that ensues from this means that new language may be quickly forgotten and that motivation may dip if children do not feel successful. This does not mean that teachers are powerless – on the contrary, providing rich input, opportunities for interaction and explanations (where children are old enough to be receptive) are all important, as are revisiting vocabulary and grammatical topics. Crucially, too, teachers need to draw children's attention to their developing language *repertoire*.

CHAPTER SUMMARY

In this chapter, we have considered children experiencing consecutive or successive bilingualism, be that as learners in a foreign-language classroom or as speakers of other languages learning the language of schooling. With the latter, we took the time to explore a little of what this entails and what the later stages of language learning might involve, including the acquisition of literacy. We have seen that the age of acquisition is a major issue in research and in forming policy decisions. With reference to the process of acquisition, we considered the role of the first language and some of the factors that may affect the rate of progress in a new language.

REFERENCES

Birdsong, D. and Molis, M. (2001) On the evidence for maturational constraints on second-language acquisition. *Journal of Memory and Language*, 44, 235–49.

Canagarajah, S. (2009) The plurilingual tradition and the English language in South Asia. In L. Lim and E. Low (eds), *Multilingual, Globalizing Asia: Implications for Policy and Education. AILA Review*. Amsterdam: John Benjamins, 5–22.

Chamot, A.U. and Harris, V. (eds) (2019) *Learning Strategy Instruction in the Language Classroom: Issues and Implementation*. Bristol: Multilingual Matters.

Council of Europe (2018) *Common European Framework of Reference for Languages: Learning, Teaching, Assessment, Companion Volume with New Descriptors*. Strasbourg: Council of Europe.

Cummins, J. (1979) Linguistic interdependence and the educational development of bilingual children. *Review of Educational Research*, 49(2), 222–51.

Cummins, J. (1980) The cross-lingual dimensions of language proficiency: implications for bilingual education and the optimal age issue. *TESOL Quarterly*, 14(2), 175–87.

Cummins, J. (1981) Linguistic interdependence and the educational development of bilingual. children. *Review of Educational Research*, 49, 222–51.

Cummins, J (1984) *Bilingualism and Special Education: Issues in Assessment and Pedagogy*. Clevedon: Multilingual Matters.

Cummins, J. (2000) *Language, Power and Pedagogy*. Clevedon: Multilingual Matters.

Curdt-Christiansen, X.L. and Huang, J. (2020) Factors influencing family language policy. In A. Shalley and S. Eisenchlas (eds), *Handbook of Social and Affective Factors in Home Language Maintenance and Development*. Berlin: De Gruyter Mouton, 174–93.

Curtiss, S., Fromkin, V., Krashen, S., Rigler, D. and Rigler, M. (1974) The linguistic development of Genie. *Language*, 50(3), 528–54.

Donaldson, M. (1978) *Children's Minds*. London: Fontana.

Drury, R. (2004) Samia and Sadaqat play school: early bilingual literacy at home. In E. Gregory, S. Long and D. Volk (eds) *Many Pathways to Literacy: Young Children Learning with Siblings, Grandparents, Peers and Communities*. London: RoutledgeFalmer.

Drury, R. (2013) How silent is the 'silent period' for young bilinguals in early years settings in England? *European Early Childhood Education Research Journal*, 21(3), 380–91. DOI: 10.1080/1350293X.2013.814362

Dyers, C. (2013) Multilingualism in late-modern Africa: identity, mobility and multivocality. *International Journal of Bilingualism*, 19(2), 1–10.

Enever, J. (2011) *ELLiE, Early Language Learning in Europe*. London: British Council.

European Commission (2008) *Communication from the Commission to the European Parliament, the Council, the European Economic and Social Committee and the Committee of the Regions – Multilingualism: An Asset for Europe and a Shared Commitment (COM(2008) 566 final)*. http://ec.europa.eu/transparency/regdoc/rep/1/2008/EN/1-2008-566-EN-F1-1.Pdf (accessed 16 March 2019).

Gibbons, J. (1985) The silent period: an examination. *Language Learning*, 35(2), 255–67.

Grenfell, M. and Harris, V. (2017) *Language Learner Strategies: Contexts, Issues and Applications in Second Language Learning and Teaching*. London: Bloomsbury.

Hamel, R.E. (2013) Language policy and ideology in Latin America. In R. Bayley, R. Cameron and C. Lucas (eds), *The Oxford Handbook of Sociolinguistics*. Oxford: Blackwell, 1–24.

Johnson, J.S. and Newport, E.L. (1989) Critical period effects in second language learning: the influence of maturational state on the acquisition of English as a second language. *Cognitive Psychology*, 21(1), 60–99.

Lenneberg, E. (1967) *The Biological Foundations of Language*. New York: Wiley.

Long, M.H. (1990) Maturational constraints on language development. *Studies in Second Language Acquisition*, 12, 251–86.

Martin-Jones M., Blackledge, A. and Creese, A. (eds) (2012) *The Routledge Handbook of Multilingualism*. London: Routledge.

Mistry, M. and Sood, K. (2020) *Meeting the Needs of Young Children with English as an Additional Language: Research Informed Practice*. London: David Fulton.

Murphy, V. (2015) *Second Language Learning in Early School Years: Trends and Contexts*. Oxford: Oxford University Press.

Nippold, M.A. (2016) *Later Language Development: School-Age Children, Adolescents, and Young Adults*. 4th edn. Austin, TX: Pro-Ed. Inc.

O'Rourke, B. (2011) Negotiating multilingualism in an Irish primary school context. In C. Hélot and M. Ó Laoire (eds), *Language Policy for the Multilingual Classroom: Pedagogy of the Possible*. Bristol: Multilingual Matters, 107–27.

Ortega, L. (2009) *Understanding Second Language Acquisition*. London: Hodder Education.

Panayi, P. (2020) *Migrant City: A New History of London*. New Haven: Yale University Press.

Panayiotou, A., Gardner, A., Williams, S., Zucchi, E., Mascitti-Meuter, M., Goh, A.M.Y., You, E., Chong, T.W.H., Logiudice, D., Lin, X., Haralambous, B. and Batchelor, F. (2019) Language translation apps in health care settings: expert opinion. *JMIR mHealth and uHealth*, 7(4), e11316. (Note: The *Journal of Medical Internet Research* is a peer-reviewed open-access medical journal established in 1999 covering eHealth and 'healthcare in the Internet age'. The editor-in-chief is Gunther Eysenbach. The publisher is JMIR.)

Penfield, W. and Roberts, L. (1959) *Speech and Brain Mechanisms*. Princeton, NJ: Princeton University Press.

Roberts, T.A. (2014) Not so silent after all: examination and analysis of the silent stage in childhood second language acquisition. *Early Childhood Research Quarterly*, 29(1), 22–-40.

Saville-Troike, M. (1988) Private speech: evidence for second language learning strategies during the 'silent' period. *Journal of Child Language*, 15(3), 567–90.

Singleton, D. and Ryan, L. (2004) *Language Acquisition: The Age Factor*. 2nd edn. Bristol: Multilingual Matters.

Snow, C and Hoefnagel-Höhle, M. (1978) Age differences in second language acquisition. In Hatch, E (ed.), *Second Language Acquisition: A Book of Readings*. Rowley, MA: Newbury House.

Swan, M. and Smith, B. (2001) *Learner English: A Guide to Interference and Other Problems*. 2nd edn. Cambridge: Cambridge University Press.

Unsworth, S. and Hulk, A. (2009) Early successive bilingualism: disentangling the relevant factors. *Zeitschrift für Sprachwissenschaft*, 28, 69–77. doi 10.1515/ZFSW.2009.008

Wong-Fillmore, L. (1979) Individual differences in second language acquisition. In C. Fillmore, D. Kempler and W. Wang (eds), *Individual Differences in Language Ability and Language Behavior*. New York: Academic Press, 203–28.

PART IV

ATYPICAL LANGUAGE DEVELOPMENT

7

ATYPICAL LANGUAGE DEVELOPMENT: SENSORY, AND SOCIAL IMPAIRMENTS

In earlier sections of this book, we have explored what kind of development path is typically followed by young children learning to talk, be that as a monolingual or as a bi- or plurilingual speaker. However, it is often the case that this typical path is not, in fact, followed and this can be due to a range of factors. 'Speech, language and communication needs' (SLCN) is an umbrella term used in the UK to describe the difficulties that some children and young people experience with language development. It is estimated that up to 10 per cent of all children in the UK will have long-term, persistent SLCN, which may necessitate intervention such as speech therapy. While of this 10 per cent, 7 per cent will have this as their primary need, in the remaining 3 per cent or so the need may arise from other impairments (Communication Trust, 2011). In this chapter, we will look at how language development is affected by hearing or visual impairment or autism. In the next chapter, we will consider the implications of Specific Language Impairment (SLI), now known as Developmental Language Disorder (DLD).

HEARING IMPAIRMENT

DEGREES AND KINDS OF HEARING IMPAIRMENT

First of all, we need to dispel the myth of the 'deaf mute': it does not necessarily follow that deaf people cannot speak. They possess the same ability to produce sounds as hearing people, although, as we shall see, some may prefer to use sign rather than spoken language. Before we consider these options we need to know a little about hearing impairment itself. There are two kinds of hearing loss: **conductive** hearing loss and **prelingual** hearing loss. Let us take conductive hearing loss first –early fluctuating conductive hearing loss, most commonly caused by otitis media, an inflammation of the middle ear. As this typically affects toddlers and young children, episodes can occur and reoccur during the process of language development. Clearly the frequency and duration of such episodes may differentially affect the perception and thus the production of speech sounds. However, it is worth bearing in mind that it is not only the frequency and duration that may impact on language development but the nature of the impairment. Hearing loss impacts both the decibel level and frequencies in sound, so it is not simply a reduction in volume. Rather, as various consonants and vowels have different frequencies, the effect on individual children will vary. An audiogram is a graph which demonstrates the hearing loss across these two axes and can allow audiologists to pinpoint exactly what is affected. For example, some children with otitis media will fail to hear high frequency speech sounds such as unvoiced fricatives (e.g. /s/, /θ/, / ʃ / and /f/) and many of these play a key role grammatically – think of the role the sound /s/ plays in English in understanding third person singular, the plural and possessive. Furthermore, reduced perception of stress and intonation can interfere with conversational ability as children may not cue into whether they are being asked a question or being told to do something. In some settings, this might be mistaken for being rude or uncooperative. However, the evidence suggests that overall the effects of conductive hearing loss are probably transient and subtle, particularly where there are no other presenting issues (Klein and Rapin, 1993: 109). Nevertheless, it is important that those caring for and working with young children are aware of this common problem.

However, a more long-term issue is that of prelingual hearing loss, which is sensori-neural in nature. This is usually caused by a lesion in the cochlea, the sensory receptor in the inner era, or by damage to the auditory pathways leading to the brain (Mogford, 1993: 113). While this often means that a baby is born deaf, in some cases babies experience neural damage through illness or degeneration in the first eighteen months of life. Thus the term 'prelingual' is preferred to congenital. There are numerous causes of this kind of hearing loss, including prematurity, infection such as measles during pregnancy or genetic causes. The extent to which children experience other problems (e.g. associated with low birth weight due to prematurity) may affect the degree and profile of hearing loss. As in the case of conductive hearing loss, there will be different frequencies and decibel levels affected and the degree of residual hearing will vary. But how does all this affect language development?

DEVELOPING SPOKEN LANGUAGE

There are choices to be made here, between **oral language** development and **sign language**. One key factor is the environment into which the baby is born. The vast majority of prelingually deaf babies are born to hearing parents (Cole and Flexer, 2020; Mogford, 1993), which may come as a surprise to the reader, given that genetic factors are sometimes present. But what this means in terms of bringing up a baby to learn sign language is that the parents are not initially in a position to provide the necessary input. Sign languages are as complex and nuanced as spoken languages. A parallel here is to imagine that as a parent you speak no French, but your baby needs to learn it! This means that many hearing parents will expose their babies to spoken language first, encouraging them to lip-read. Brookes and Kempe (2012: 240), however, point to the difficulty of acquiring a spoken language successfully for a profoundly deaf child, and suggest that many children in this situation do not encounter sign language until they are of school age. What makes the development of spoken language so challenging? During the first year, establishing joint attention is difficult. In hearing children, parents can point to an item, draw the child's attention to it and name it, so that the child simultaneously sees it and hears its name. With deaf babies, this triangular arrangement is effectively broken in that, while the caregiver can point to an item and draw the child's attention to it, the spoken word(s) cannot be heard and it may not be possible for the baby to look at the parent's mouth at the same time as the object. Unsurprisingly, first words can be delayed and vocabulary smaller. Deaf babies tend to babble at the same time as hearing babies, but then stop – they cannot hear themselves, so they receive no feedback. As noted above in the case of conductive hearing loss, high frequency loss affects consonants such as /s/ with the concomitant effect on grammar, and problems with stress and intonation affect conversational interaction. Also, in English, it can be difficult to perceive unstressed syllables and many crucial pieces of the language 'jigsaw', such as modal auxiliaries, are often in unstressed syllables. An utterance such as 'I could've eaten that' effectively hides the 'have' from hearing children so it is easy to imagine how hearing loss can render this task all the more difficult. Deaf children find not only auxiliaries difficult, but also sentences that do not follow SVO (subject, verb, object). Questions, negatives, relative clauses and pronoun use also throw up challenges (De Villiers *et al.*, 1994). At later stages, problems with clarification requests or providing information may be problematic. Matching linguistic and cognitive development may also prove problematic, as children (due to smaller vocabulary and difficulty with understanding word meanings) may not have the linguistic means of expressing themselves on a par with their developing cognition. A final consideration takes us back to the input, as deaf children cannot 'overhear' – that is, for example, they cannot listen in to a dialogue between two people and infer how questions and answers 'fit' together. So is the answer to develop sign language? While there are choices to be made, this is not clear-cut. Decisions will vary according to the age of diagnosis, the technology available and the family situation. Where hearing parents opt for speaking to their child, they may at the same time supplement this with signs and gesture; in some cases children may use something called 'home sign', essentially creating signs based on objects and activities. However, **technological advances** in the last few decades have proved beneficial to the development of speaking skills. Contemporary hearing aids are increasingly sophisticated, although variable sensitivity to sound means that the use of these can be limited. A key breakthrough has been the invention of cochlear implants that can provide a sense of hearing to children with a functioning auditory nerve. Indeed, according to Cole and Flexer (2020: 12), technology can provide access to the entire speech spectrum even for children with profound hearing loss. It is increasingly common for these to be fitted when children are between seven and twelve months old and, while the degree of hearing loss is related to outcomes, the age of implementation is the most significant variable. In fact, Cole and Flexer (2020: 15) suggest that where a spoken language is the desired outcome by the parents, implementation should happen in the first few weeks of life. Nevertheless, there are those who argue for an early introduction to sign language.

DEVELOPING SIGN LANGUAGE

Brookes and Kempe argue that earlier exposure to sign language is beneficial and that age of first exposure is the key factor in fluency in production and comprehension of sign language (Brookes and Kempe, 2012: 246). Not only this, they further suggest that 'native signers' have an advantage in acquiring a spoken language and in learning to read and write. This can address the concerns that some may have that children who sign do not then have the motivation to learn spoken language. Of course, although some parents and family members may over time develop some competence in sign language, this will be by no means all and children naturally want to communicate within their social context and later function in a speaking world. Encouragingly, Brookes and Kempe go on to say that native-signing deaf children can become fluent bilinguals. But how do children acquire a sign language?

Let us consider what exactly a **sign language** is. First of all, sign languages do not 'replace' spoken languages – indeed, we need to shake off the assumption that language is inseparable from speech (Armstrong *et al.*, 1995: 66). Clearly sign languages use a visual-spatial (sometimes called visual-gestural) modality rather than an auditory one. A sign can therefore simultaneously convey a verb meaning *and* past tense whereas spoken language is linear – that is, even if it is just one word (e.g. 'walked') one morpheme has to follow the other in real time. This means that sign languages have grammars that are distinct from spoken ones. Individual signs are composed of five elements that can be remembered using the acronym HOLME: Hand shape (palm), Orientation, Location (place of articulation), Movement and (facial) Expression. As each of these aspects can be articulated in numerous ways, one sign can be differentiated from another (Brookes and Kempe, 2012: 241). It is also important to note that sign languages are not simply manual gestures but also employ facial expressions and upper body positions that replace the prosody (stress and intonation) of spoken language. In terms of vocabulary, lexical items in sign languages are more iconic than in spoken languages – apart from onomatopoetic forms, spoken language does not really have a relationship between the concept and the linguistic form. Information is conveyed differently between sign and spoken language – something that has already been mentioned is that more than one concept can be signalled at the same time. A final consideration is that there are multiple sign languages such that, for example, American Sign Language and British Sign Language are not mutually intelligible.

So how is sign language acquired? Let us think first of all about the timing of acquisition. One thing to bear in mind is the variation with which deaf babies may be exposed to models of sign language. That said, what is striking is the degree of similarity to the process of acquiring spoken language: deaf babies do babble orally and then, lacking feedback, tend to tail off; but those acquiring sign language 'babble' with their hands, proceeding to single signs and then sign combinations – at more or less the same time as hearing babies proceed to combining more than one spoken word. Like hearing babies, their signs are initially approximations and practice is needed for more target-like forms to be produced. There may, however, be differences related to the age of acquisition.

DEAF BABIES AND DEAF PARENTS

In a minority of cases, deaf babies have sign language exposure from their parents from birth. Research suggests that the rate of development is broadly similar to the rate of development of spoken language in hearing babies (Messer, 1994), although the appearance of signs has been noted to be a little earlier than spoken words, at possibly eight months of age rather than ten or twelve months. This may be because the motor prerequisites for hand movements are less complex than those for vocal articulation or possibly because parents may be able to shape their children's hands in a way they cannot exercise influence over their articulators (see Messer, 1994). Messer further suggests that deaf parents may modify signs for children and also facilitate their acquisition by gaining the child's attention, as well as signing in the child's visual field. It is difficult to classify signs as all babies gesture in some way (reaching out for a toy, for example) and imitate their caregivers, so some may be routines or imitations. There is some evidence that referential signs – that is, those naming/referring to an object – only appear later, at around twelve months – the same time as words are used referentially in spoken language. This suggests that there is an underlying cognitive element to language acquisition.

DEAF BABIES AND HEARING PARENTS

We have already seen that this represents the majority of cases, and that the development of oral language is not without its problems, although technology such as cochlear implants and more sophisticated hearing aids can mitigate the impact of hearing loss. Brookes and Kempe, however, argue that public health education should aim to inform parents of deaf children of the importance of early introduction of sign language (2012: 247). Grosjean (2001) suggests that sign language should be a child's first language, but also that deaf children have the right to grow up bilingually, although he notes that one language may be dominant depending on the family context. Some children may, of course, find themselves in a bilingual environment, with one hearing and one deaf parent. Age of first exposure to sign language appears to be key and can impact all aspects of sign language acquisition and processing – prosodic, phonological, lexical, morphological and syntactic Furthermore, Brookes and Kempe (2012: 247–8) report that there are cognitive implications for late signers in that they do not develop theory of mind (see Chapter 1) in the same way as either early (native) signers or hearing children. Arguably, without full access to either spoken language or sign language input, children are at risk of not having real exposure to *language*. We noted above that children may develop something called 'home sign'. There is some evidence that in these circumstances children are developing a linguistic system of their own. Research points to a non-random use of gestures by deaf children of hearing parents (Goldin-Meadow and Myland, 1990). In the absence of external structured input, they may be acquiring a systematic way of communicating with others (see Messer, 1994).

HEARING CHILDREN OF DEAF PARENTS

A final consideration is the hearing children of deaf parents. Research suggests that some of these children develop language in a typical way, whereas others experience some difficulty or delay (Schiff-Myers, 1993). This is a complex situation, as some deaf parents may communicate through sign language, some orally or some a mixture of both. This means that the hearing child may experience limited exposure to spoken language, which may also have characteristics of the spoken language of deaf people (see above for some of the issues that affect the development of spoken language). The child may start to develop sign language and/or realise that their parents' communication is different from others'. Factors such as the presence of speaking siblings, grandparents and other family members will affect the amount of exposure and opportunity for oral interaction for individual children. We might here reiterate Grosjean's point that children have the right to grow up bilingually, and note that, particularly where the parents are sign-language users, children will acquire sign language and spoken language simultaneously. This means their bilingualism is **bimodal**. We saw earlier how sign language and oral language have different modalities. What is fascinating is that, compared with unimodal bilingual children who acquire two spoken languages, these children are able to produce signs and spoken words at the same time and therefore are not obliged to suppress one language during the production process of a code-mixed utterance (Kanto *et al*., 2017). Kanto *et al*. also found in a study of eight children from the age of twelve to 36 months that their code-mixing was systematic and concluded that parents of bilingual children and professionals working with them need to consider code-mixing as a natural sign of linguistic and communicative competence (2017: 962). This, of course, can equally apply to deaf babies of hearing parents (see above), although the age of exposure to sign language may vary.

To summarise thus far, language development and deafness present a complex picture. Variables such as whether parents are deaf or not and the availability and suitability of technology affect decisions as to whether oral language development or sign language should be prioritised. Given that bilingual competence is seen by many as an ideal outcome, the findings that those children who are native/early signers develop spoken language more successfully point to the need to provide early support for this.

VISUAL IMPAIRMENT

DEGREES AND KINDS OF VISUAL IMPAIRMENT

While the impact of a hearing impairment is immediately obvious, the effect of visual impairment is perhaps less so, at least at first. But as we shall discover, there are implications that arise from problems with vision. Like hearing impairment, however, visual impairment is not a uniform issue. There are different kinds of impairment, such as loss of central vision, loss of peripheral vision, blurred vision and extreme light sensitivity. Vision impairment can range from no vision – blindness – or very low vision to not being able to see particular colours. According to the Royal National Institute for the Blind (RNIB), 'severely sight-impaired' means that you are *blind* and 'sight-impaired' means that you are *partially sighted* (https://www.rnib.org.uk/eye-health/registering-your-sight-loss/criteria-certification). Babies can be born blind, possibly as a result of genetic factors or related to prematurity. Others acquire it later, as a result of disease, injury or a medical condition; a further issue is its coincidence with other problems. Messer (1994: 254) suggests that blind children who do not have other disabilities appear to acquire language at much the same rate as sighted children, but that there are nevertheless subtle differences between the speech of blind and sighted children. In the following section, we will focus on children blind from birth. Those who initially have vision and then lose it may, of course, benefit from this brief exposure.

SOUNDS AND WORDS

We saw in Chapter 3 how important that first year of life is in developing preverbal communication. Clearly, children who are blind from birth are unable to benefit from the triangular arrangement of a parent pointing out and naming an item, but this time because they cannot see the thing being referred to. The importance of **mutual gaze** in parent–child interaction is well established (see Butterworth, 2004; Niedźwiecka *et al.*, 2018) and given the importance of social interaction in language development there are implications for the blind child. They cannot see the person who is speaking, so that sound perception and production is affected. We know that blind and sighted children tend to babble at the same age, but it appears that there are differences related to the visibility of mouth movements – sounds like /p/, /b/ and /m/ are produced at the front of the mouth and blind children produce more errors than sighted children with these, whereas sounds that are less observable such as /k/ and /g/ at the back of the mouth are acquired in the same way irrespective of sightedness. This may also result in blind children having fewer words in their vocabulary that have visible mouth movements than sighted children (Messer, 1994: 254). The vocabulary of blind children may also differ in other ways. For example, everyday household items may feature more than animals do – these are things than can be physically handled, whereas many children learn the names of animals from picture books, notably those animals that they are unlikely to encounter in the local park! Other items that can cause difficulty are large items that cannot be simultaneously experienced. If you think about a car, a sighted person can take in all of the features at once: height, length, colour, shininess, items such as doors and wheels; in a blind person, these can only be experienced sequentially. Other things that are at a distance such as clouds and mountains are also tricky and items that are fragile (glass) or dangerous (fire) can also pose problems, not least of all for a parent trying to keep a child safe. Of course, blind children have other senses to rely upon, including auditory, olfactory and gustatory as well as haptic, the ability to identify things by touch.

There is also some evidence that blind children may underextend the meaning of words, limiting them to individual items – although sighted children also do this. However, it may be that blind children have fewer opportunities to observe the characteristics that are shared among different things. Consequently, categorising and classifying things may be more difficult for blind than sighted children. Personal pronouns present a problem often noted in the speech of blind children, as these are often reversed, so that 'you want a drink' may be used as a request for one, as if the specific meanings of pronouns such as 'I' and 'you' are yet to be learned. Similarly, deictic terms such as 'here' and 'there' may pose problems as it is difficult to judge distances, and locational terms such as prepositions of place (in, on) can also be tricky. Other terms that are tricky are what we call 'sighted terms' such as 'see' and 'look'. Mills (1993: 158) suggests that children may use these with the meaning of 'hear' and that their interpretation and use may be context dependent.

SOCIAL INTERACTION

Mills notes the conflicting evidence in relation to morphology and syntax, and suggests that where there is a delay it may be for reasons other than the visual impairment. For example, there is some evidence that auxiliary verbs may be delayed but that this may be explained by parents using fewer of them, preferring to give direct instructions/imperatives. Indeed, there may be other differences in the input, as some research suggests fewer descriptions and more labels in the input, with a concomitant increase in the use of labels by blind children themselves. The issue of the input, of course, brings us back to social interaction. A key issue here is that of **attention-getting**. Whereas sighted children use a variety of strategies to gain someone's attention, such as eye contact and directing their interlocutor's attention to something by gaze, blind children have to use other means such as touching and calling out/using names. Mills (1993: 160) suggests that it takes time for blind children to learn the appropriate use of such strategies (perhaps pinching someone instead) and that at times their attempts may be unsuccessful as the child is unable to assess the chances of the listener hearing them. She points out how important it is that blind children should not be discouraged from initiating communication. Questions are another way of gaining attention and blind children may use these more often than sighted children as a way of entering conversation; they may continue to do this for a longer time than sighted children, also using them as a way of changing topic. This is also something more frequently done by blind children as they have fewer cues for determining if their listener is still paying attention. A final consideration is that some children display echolalia, or repetition of words and phrases. Although more commonly associated with autism (see below), this aspect of some blind children's speech may simply reflect a good rote memory and/or difficulty in breaking down the event sequences that are related to language.

To summarise this section, it appears that blind children in general develop spoken language successfully, albeit with some subtle differences. These are important to bear in mind in order to provide a facilitative environment for language and communication to flourish.

AUTISM

WHAT IS AUTISM?

Autism is a lifelong developmental disability, first identified by child psychiatrist Leo Kanner in 1943, who noted a group of young children whose interactions were characterised by social aloofness, interest in objects, like of sameness and difficulties with communication. He noted repetition, problems with pronouns and a literal approach to language. Later, Hans Asperger (1944), a Viennese paediatrician, focused on a group of individuals who shared autistic characteristics but were apparently high-functioning, with higher than average intelligence and no history of language delay. For some years, Asperger's syndrome was used as a description of such individuals, the term introduced by Lorna Wing in 1981 in the UK (Wing, 1981), and one still used in Europe (Baron-Cohen, 2017). The range of individuals who fall into some classification of autism, however, is such that it is more appropriate to think of a spectrum. The American Psychiatric Association (APA, 2013) diagnostic term is 'autism spectrum disorder' (ASD). However, the umbrella term 'autism spectrum condition' (ASC) is considered by many to be less stigmatising as it embraces not only impairments, but strengths as well (NASEN, 2016). This is the term we will use in this book. While the primary focus of the book is the development of language, this, of course, needs to be understood within the context of other issues. So it is worth having an understanding of the key characteristics of autism. For a long time, these were thought to consist of a triad of impairments (Wing and Gould, 1979): first, difficulties with social and emotional understanding;

second, inflexibility of thought and behaviour; and, third, problems with communication and language. More recently, American Psychiatric Association *Diagnostic and Statistical Manual of Mental Disorders* (5th edn, 2013), known as DSM-5, has proposed a dyad whereby the previous triad is condensed into two elements: social and communication deficits; and restricted and repetitive patterns of behaviour, interests, or activities.

What do these characteristics mean in practice? Problems with the social and communicative aspects of life might mean that an autistic child may not understand why someone is upset; or, they have difficulty 'reading' the expressions on someone's face to arrive at that interpretation. They may have difficulty acquiring the social skills that are deemed culturally appropriate for the society they live in. What about restricted and repetitive patterns of behaviour, interests, or activities? These can manifest themselves in a number of ways. For example, routines may be strictly adhered to, such that in many autistic people any deviation causes acute distress. Then some children need to follow exactly the same route to school every day, which may include touching particular milestones on the route; less obviously, some will want to wear exactly the same clothes every day or will insist on a particular kind of drink, toothpaste or bedtime routine. Of course, most in the neuro-typical world will also have certain habits and preferences (a favourite sweater, a particular route around the supermarket) and this is a reminder to us all that this *is* indeed a spectrum. Particularly with younger children, however, failure to stick rigidly to these habits can cause severe distress, and combined with the sensory overload that many autistic people experience – noise that seems too loud, colour displays in shops, material that feels too tickly – can result in what may appear to be a tantrum, but is in fact a meltdown, signalling that they are overwhelmed. As children get older, many learn strategies that help them cope with these situations, but the stress may be internalised and quiet time needed to recover. Those with ASC may also have very keen interests in particular topics and with this comes the ability to focus very intently, which is one of the clear strengths of autistic people. Possibly related to this is the idea of 'islets of often remarkable skill or talent' (Fay, 1993: 191); while manifestations of this more typically include the ability to memorise – lists of names, bus timetables and so on, often related to particular obsessions or hobbies – there are also reported instances of remarkable skills in say, mathematics, art or music. One well-known example of this is the artist Stephen Wiltshire, whose ability to produce detailed drawings after only brief exposure to them is quite staggering (www. https://www.stephenwiltshire.co.uk). This aspect of autism was memorably captured by Dustin Hoffman's portrayal of an autistic man in the 1988 film *Rain Man*. But in reality, these are the exceptions rather than the rule. They do, however, reflect the ability of the autistic brain (to a greater or lesser degree) to give a high degree of focus to something of import. Autism is also associated with cognitive strengths, notably in domains such as excellent attention to detail, excellent memory for detail and a strong drive to detect patterns (Baron-Cohen, 2006).

That we now recognise the potential strengths of autistic people challenges the notion of a disorder. More recently, many have come to embrace the notion of **neuro-diversity**, from which perspective autism is seen as an example of diversity within a range of possible brains, all of which are simply different (Silberman, 2015). There is no doubting the heterogeneous nature of ASC. At one end of this, there may be people who are unable to live independently and fail to develop language and communication, and struggle greatly with their experience of the world. Many other people on the autistic spectrum, however, are highly successful and competent people, despite the difficulties autism presents. But what individuals on this autism spectrum all share – relative to age- and IQ-matched individuals without autism – are the social communication difficulties, difficulties with cognitive empathy or theory of mind, the difficulties adjusting to unexpected change, a love of repetition or 'need for sameness', unusually narrow interests and sensory hyper- and hyposensitivities (Baron-Cohen, 2006).

What is the **prevalence** of autism? According to the National Autistic Society, one person in every 100 is within ASC; in the UK, there are about 700,000 autistic children and adults (National Autistic Society, n.d.b). One difficulty is that many children and adults who might fit the criteria are often undiagnosed as their difficulties are ascribed to something else. The prevalence of autism among boys was noted by both Kanner and Asperger (who initially thought only boys had it) and the National Autistic Society estimates that the current ratio is four males to every female, although this is an average figure (NASEN, 2016). Recent research, however, suggests that girls and young women are much more likely than boys or men to miss out on a diagnosis. Among other theories, it may be that women and girls are better at masking or camouflaging their difficulties or indeed that autism traits in girls are under-reported by teachers (see NASEN, 2016). There may therefore be children in your care who are undiagnosed.

AUTISM AND LANGUAGE

How does this affect language development? Children with autism may have varying degrees of difficulty acquiring speech and language, but social communication difficulties are a cardinal feature for diagnosing autism (Prelock and Nelson, 2012: 129). We noted earlier in this chapter the importance of mutual gaze and joint attention. Prelock and Nelson note that young children who are diagnosed with autism are less likely to use joint attention acts and gestures and are less able to coordinate their vocalisations, eye gaze and gesture. They also caution that it is more difficult to make a diagnosis at two to three years because early delays in saying first words, establishing joint attention and engaging socially may be attributed to normal variation, whereas at five to six years discrepancies from normal development are more obvious. They go on, however, to stress the importance of caregivers' awareness of typical language development (2012: 133–4). The language of those with autism, variation notwithstanding, often displays certain characteristics. In terms of language, autism is fundamentally a pragmatic disorder (see Chapter 2), where the social use of language is impaired. Fay (1993: 201) suggests that pragmatic problems permeate every aspect of the verbal development of autistic children. One characteristic is known as **echolalia**. This can be immediate, involving repetition of language just heard, including questions; it can also be delayed and reproduced at a time when the reference is not clear. This may be related to problems with speaker roles, something else noted with autistic people. They may use an unanalysed utterance to express a feeling – for example, 'it's ok, he won't hurt you' to express anxiety, or questions such as 'do you want a biscuit?' to request one. We noted in Chapter 3 that some typically developing young children use unanalysed routines, but this tends to develop into structured speech without difficulties. While the example above is sometimes seen as pronoun reversal, in fact it suggests a difficulty in breaking down and analysing language (see Chapter 1) in order to extract and reorder the component parts of it. We might speculate here that this represents a parallel with the inability some autistic people have to break down event sequences and their struggle with variations to established routines. On a positive note, it may be the child's attempt to maintain communication (Fay, 1993: 196).

Some have noted other problems with phonology, typically the monotone nature of some children's utterances and also a tendency to retain a parent's accent rather than adopting that of peers when they start school (Attwood, 1998: 79). Problems with perception tend to be at the level of prosody, affecting perception of stress, rhythm and intonation. This in turn affects the ability to recognise language functions such as sarcasm or irony, or to see the intention behind teasing. Prosodic problems can also affect grammar, where, in English, stress on different words can change the meaning intended – compare, for example, '*I* didn't say I liked chips' to 'I didn't say I *liked* chips'. Implied and multiple meanings can serve to confuse the autistic child. Thus, autistic people often have a **literal *interpretation*** of the language they hear. This makes us realise how much shared knowledge aids communication between speakers. Autistic people are more likely to interpret language literally. For example, when someone directs us to wipe our feet, we do not remove our socks and shoes, whereas a severely autistic child might. The use of metaphor in language is also potentially confusing such as 'I'm roasting' Even highly successful autistic people can follow instructions to the letter to their detriment: one bright autistic graduate failed to realise that the instruction 'spray with water' was insufficient to keep a plant alive – because it didn't actually say 'and water the plant'!

The difficulties outlined above point to problems interpreting the beliefs and intentions of other people. This has led some to propose that autistic individuals lack a theory of mind, suggesting that children with autism fail to develop the ability to think about mental states in the normal way, and thus fail to understand behaviour in terms of mental states (Frith, 1989; Baron-Cohen *et al.*, 1994). They may have difficulty conceptualising the thoughts and feelings of others, and fail to appreciate that a comment could cause offence or embarrassment (Attwood, 1998: 112).

CONVERSATION

The art of conversation is something many of us take for granted, failing to recognise the subtlety and sophistication of this. Neuro-typical children gradually learn (see Chapter 3) to initiate dialogue, maintain communication, take turns and interrupt appropriately. They also learn to read visual and auditory cues that signal a speaker is trying to finish a conversation, is bored, or wanting to make a point. We learn the art of changing the subject, bringing a conversation to a close or judging how much time it is suitable to talk for. Autistic people find these rules of conversation difficult. As one young woman we know put it, 'I finally realised that other people know something that I don't.' Problems with interaction exist alongside other elements of autism, such as the well-attested tendency of autistic people to have particular interests or even obsessions. On the one hand, this may furnish them with a sophisticated lexicon about their particular passion; on the other hand, they may need to learn that not everyone will share this and/or be willing to listen at length. We also learn the art of 'phatic communion' (Malinowski, 1923), the use of language to maintain relationships with other people. Think how often we use phrases such as: *how's tricks? Lovely day isn't it? How was your holiday?* We do not necessarily *need* to communicate about any of this. Many autistic people fail to see the point of this. This, like other conversational skills, has to be learned and many will learn simply by copying others. A further issue is related to the need for routine in that an autistic child may seek reassurance about what is happening by asking questions: 'what are we doing next?' is a question that has exasperated more than one parent of an autistic child that we know. Or it did, until the penny dropped that this was not a request for further activity, but quite literally an enquiry about what would happen next. As Attwood (1998: 81) points out, lack of precision is difficult for the autistic child to tolerate, so that it may be necessary to avoid words such as 'perhaps' and 'maybe'; sometimes, he notes, the child will 'bombard' a speaker with questions seeking reassurance about when an event will occur.

What about autistic children in a childcare or classroom setting? Children who already have a diagnosis will have benefited from a clear description of their language profile; but there may be children in your care who display some of the characteristics outlined above. Some children, notably girls (Dworzynski *et al.*, 2012), may master strategies that 'mask' the autistic experience and their language may be deceptively sophisticated in terms of grammar and vocabulary. As teachers, we need to be alert to the more subtle difficulties that they may be experiencing, while bearing in mind the width of the autistic spectrum.

To summarise this section, then, autistic spectrum disorder is a lifelong disability that impairs communication and social interaction. The spectrum encompasses those who may need supported living as adults and those who will grow into successful and competent individuals. Awareness of their needs by professionals is key.

CHAPTER SUMMARY

In this chapter, we have been able to see some of the different ways in which children learn language. Our focus has been on the needs that arise from sensory impairment (auditory or visual) and autistic spectrum conditions. Considering how the absence of a communication channel (sight, hearing) impacts upon language development illustrates the complex way in which human beings develop language and the way in which the autistic brain works may shed light upon the some of the social and cognitive underpinnings of language.

REFERENCES

American Psychiatric Association (APA) (2013) *Diagnostic and Statistical Manual of Mental Disorders*. 5th edn. Washington, DC: APA.

Armstrong, D.F., Stokoe, W.C. and Wilcox, S.E. (1995) *Gesture and the Nature of Language*. Cambridge: Cambridge University Press.

Asperger, H. (1944) Die 'autistischen Psychopathen' im Kindesalter. *Archiv fur Psychiatrie und Nervenkrankheiten*, 117, 76–136.

Attwood, T. (1998) *Asperger's Syndrome: A Guide for Parents and Professionals*. London: Jessica Kingsley.

Baron-Cohen, S. (2006) Two new theories of autism: hyper-systemizing and assortative mating. *Archives of Diseases in Childhood*, 91, 2–5.

Baron-Cohen, S. (2017) Editorial perspective: neurodiversity – a revolutionary concept for autism and psychiatry. *Journal of Child Psychology and Psychiatry*. 58(6), 744–7.

Baron-Cohen, S., Tager-Flusberg, H. and Cohen, D.J. (eds) (1994) *Understanding Other Minds: Perspectives from Autism*. Oxford: Oxford University Press.

Brookes, P.J. and Kempe, V. (2012) *Language Development*. Oxford: Blackwell.

Butterworth, G. (2004) Joint visual attention in infancy. In G. Bremner and A. Fogel (eds), *Blackwell Handbook of Infant Development*. Malden, MA: Blackwell, 213–40.

Cole, E.B. and Flexer, C.A. (2020) *Children with Hearing Loss: Developing Listening and Talking, Birth to Six*. 4th edn. San Diego, CA: Plural.

Communication Trust (2011) *Don't Get Me Wrong: Information for Supporting Children and Young People with Speech, Language and Communication Needs*. Available at: https://www.thecommunicationtrust.org.uk/media/174/dontgetme-wrong.pdf (accessed 2 October 2020).

De Villiers, J., De Villiers, P. and Hoban, E. (1994) The central problem of functional categories in the English syntax of oral deaf children. In Tager-Flusberg, H. (ed.), *Constraints on Language Acquisition*. Hove: Lawrence Erlbaum, 9–48.

Dworzynski, K., Ronald, A., Bolton, P. and Happé, F. (2012) How different are girls and boys above and below the diagnostic threshold for autism spectrum disorders? *Journal of the American Academy of Child and Adolescent Psychiatry*, 51(8), 788–97.

Fay, W.H. (1993) Infantile autism. In D. Bishop and K. Mogford (eds), *Language Development in Exceptional Circumstances*. Hove: Lawrence Erlbaum, 190–202.

Frith, U. (1989) *Autism: Explaining the Enigma*. Oxford: Basil Blackwell.

Goldin-Meadow, S. and Mylander, C. (1990) The role of parental input in the development of a morphological system. *Journal of Child Language*, 17, 527–63.

Grosjean, F. (2001) The right of the deaf child to grow up bilingual. *Sign Language Studies*, 1(2), 110–14.

Kanner, L. (1943) Autistic disturbances of affective contact. *The Nervous Child*, 2(2), 217–50.

Kanto, L., Laakso, M. and Huttunen, K. (2017) Use of code-mixing by young hearing children of deaf parents. *Bilingualism: Language and Cognition*, 20(5), 947–64.

Klein, S.K. and Rapin, I. (1993) Intermittent conductive hearing loss and language impairment. In D. Bishop and K. Mogford (eds), *Language Development in Exceptional Circumstances*. Hove: Lawrence Erlbaum, 96–109.

Malinowski, B. (1923) The problem of meaning in primitive languages. In C.K. Ogden and I.A. Richards (eds), *The Meaning of Meaning*. London: Kegan Paul, Trench and Trubner, 296–336.

Messer, D. (1994) *The Development of Communication: From Social Interaction to Language*. Chichester: John Wiley & Sons.

Mills, A. (1993) Visual handicap. In D. Bishop and K. Mogford (eds), *Language Development in Exceptional Circumstances*. Hove: Lawrence Erlbaum, 150–64.

Mogford, K. (1993) Oral language development in the pre-linguistically deaf. In D. Bishop and K. Mogford (eds), *Language Development in Exceptional Circumstances*. Hove: Lawrence Erlbaum, 110–31.

NASEN (2016) *Girls and Autism: Flying Under the Radar*. A quick guide to supporting girls with autism spectrum conditions. Available at: www.nasen.org.uk (accessed 29 October 2020).

National Autistic Society (n.d.a) *What is Autism?* Available at: https://www.autism.org.uk/advice-and-guidance/what-is-autism (accessed 24 September 2020).

National Autistic Society (n.d.b) *Myths, Facts and Statistics*. Available at: https://www.autism.org.uk/advice-and-guidance/what-is-autism (accessed 3 November 2020).

Niedźwiecka, A., Ramotowska, S. and Tomalski, P. (2017) Mutual gaze during early mother–infant interactions promotes attention control development. *Child Development*, 89(6), 2230–44.

Prelock, P.J. and Nelson, N.W. (2012) Language and communication in autism: an integrated view. *The Pediatric Clinics of North America*, 59(1), 129–45.

Schiff-Myers, N. (1993) Hearing children of deaf parents. In D. Bishop and K. Mogford (eds), *Language Development in Exceptional Circumstances*. Hove: Lawrence Erlbaum, 47–61.

Silberman, S. (2015) *Neurotribes: The Legacy of Autism and how to Think Smarter about People who Think Differently*. London: Allen&Unwin.

Wing, L. (1981) Asperger's syndrome: a clinical account. *Psychological Medicine*, 11(1), 115–29.

Wing, L. and Gould, J. (1979) Severe impairments of social interaction and associated abnormalities in children. *Journal of Autism and Developmental Disorders*, 9(1), 11–29.

8

DEVELOPMENTAL LANGUAGE DISORDER

INTRODUCTION

In Chapter 7, we saw how other disabilities such as sensory impairment or autism can have an impact upon language development. Given what we know about the role of hearing, vision and social interaction, it is unsurprising that there are implications for language when such issues are present. However, there is also a group of children *without* any obvious disabilities who struggle to develop language in the usual way. Without any identifiable physical or psychological explanation, about 7 per cent of the UK population fail to develop language in a typical way, with boys slightly more likely to be affected than girls (Tomblin *et al.*, 1997). However, this does not mean that this is a homogeneous group of children. Rather, while they share delay in the acquisition of language, they may differ in their presentation. As this is a diagnosis by exclusion – that is, any other obvious explanation has been ruled out – they may differ in the causes of their language impairment (Hoff-Ginsberg, 1997: 320).

DEVELOPMENTAL LANGUAGE DISORDER

There has been much debate about the most appropriate terminology to use for children that have difficulties with expressive and/or receptive language skills. Previously, the term 'specific language impairment' (SLI) was used to denote the fact that the impairment specifically affected language (also known as developmental dysphasia in the 1970s), but the term 'developmental language disorder' is now preferred as this can permit children who do not necessarily meet the criteria for SLI to benefit from the same kinds of interventions. This was the outcome of a 2016 international group of 57 experts (the CATALISE panel) (Bishop *et al.*, 2016, 2017) meeting to agree upon this term. This applies when the language disorder is not associated with a known condition such as autism spectrum condition, brain injury, genetic conditions such as Down's syndrome and sensori-neural hearing loss. The definition also explicitly excludes children who have limited language skills because of lack of exposure to the language of instruction, although they may, of course, benefit from intervention. Confusingly perhaps, many books and articles written before this revised definition refer to SLI. Accordingly, we will use the term 'developmental language disorder' (DLD) in this chapter, but where the term SLI is used in publications, we will refer to SLI. Tomblin (2015: 527) describes SLI as one form of developmental language disorder, so we can see that the new definition is a slightly broader one which recognises the difficulty of diagnosis. A child can be diagnosed with DLD if their language difficulties are likely to carry on into adulthood, have a significant impact on progress at school, or on everyday life and are unlikely to catch up without help. Children are most often identified during the pre-school years (Leonard, 2015). Tomblin (2015: 535) suggest that SLI emerges as persisting poor language achievement during the pre-school years; further, he notes that if a child presents with this after the age of four there is a considerable likelihood that this will persist.

So, in this chapter, we will concentrate on those children who appear to have no ready explanation for the difficulties they are experiencing. How might these children present? The first thing to bear in mind here is that all those involved with young children need a firm grasp of the typical language development path that children take. By reading earlier chapters (see Chapters 3 and 4) you should by now have a fairly clear idea of what to expect of four- and five-year-old children (or younger) in your care and be able to identify cases where children are not making the progress you would expect. Of course, there may be instances of social disadvantage or general learning difficulties that can have a similar impact, which is why it is so important to have a holistic assessment of children's abilities and experiences.

In the absence of any obvious explanation, then, there will be some children who have expressive and/or receptive problems with language.

Expressive problems may include difficulty saying what they want to, even though they have ideas they want to express. They may struggle to find or remember appropriate words to express their ideas. While they may be trying to talk in sentences, these may be difficult to follow and sound confused. From a receptive point of view, they may find it difficult to understand long instructions, have difficulty remembering the words they want to say and find it hard to participate in what is going on in the playground. According to Tomblin (2015: 534–5) the principal way that children with SLI differ from other children has to do with the rate of development referenced to their chronological age; the bulk of the language features of children with SLI are quite similar to younger typically developing children. However, a child with DLD won't necessarily sound like a younger child; instead their speech might sound disorganised or unusual. This highlights the dilemma of deciding whether a child's language is **disordered** or simply **delayed**. This is a tricky one, as a child with delayed language will experience a mismatch between cognitive development and the linguistic means of expressing this, which can result in apparently atypical speech. Having said that, a significant delay would itself indicate some kind of problem. And while some children are 'late talkers', many tend to catch up with their peers quite quickly and experience no long-term problems. More recently, the idea that SLI may emerge as a sub-group of late talkers has been challenged in that normal language skills at around two years of age are also not necessarily indicative that a child will not develop SLI later in the pre-school years (Tomblin, 2015). We will return to this issue later. It is, however, worth noting that in all likelihood not all children who present as delayed necessarily have a disorder, but that children with a disorder will experience delay in acquiring communication skills that are age-appropriate.

So, as indicated above, many children with DLD, in the absence of any obvious explanation will experience receptive and/or expressive problems with language. However, as Brookes and Kempe (2012: 214) point out, more recent research is indicating that the underlying causes of what they term SLI may be more general than previously thought, involving, for example, motor control and working memory in addition to language. Next, however, we will take a closer look at the domains of language that we have previously referred to in this book, as these are not uniformly affected.

AUDITORY AND PHONOLOGICAL PROCESSING

First of all, let us look at the acquisition of the sound system. It has long been shown that children with DLD have problems with **auditory processing**. The work of Tallal and colleagues brought this to our attention in the 1970s. For example, when faced with rapidly presented stimuli of short duration, they may struggle to discriminate whether a second tone in a pair is of higher frequency or longer duration than the first tone (Tallal and Piercy, 1973). A further possibility is that children have difficulties processing prosody. Corriveau *et al.* (2007: 648) note that prosodic cues (in particular, changes in duration and stress) carry important information about how sounds are ordered into words when the words are multisyllabic. It is estimated that 90 per cent of English bisyllabic content words follow a strong–weak syllable pattern, with the stress on the first syllable (e.g. monkey, bottle, doctor, sister). Their study was carried out to examine basic auditory processing abilities related to perceiving stress and syllable prominence in a sample of children aged seven to eleven diagnosed as having SLI; the study revealed that the majority of the children had perception problems related to the amplitude and duration of syllables, leading the researchers to conclude that 'an early insensitivity to auditory cues to rhythm and stress could have profound and lasting consequences on word segmentation and the development of the language system' (2007: 663), as prosody offers clues to word segmentation and grammatical morphology. This may also have implications for research in other languages as not all languages use the same prosodic features to highlight syntactic information.

Phonological processing problems are also common in children with DLD, affecting the processing of the phonemic contrasts that are present in the language to be learned. Phonological problems must not be confused with articulatory problems, which are physical in nature. These include, for example, cleft palate, where the split in the roof of the mouth would render sounds made there difficult. Problems with phonological processing are often manifested by immature speech sounds, words that are mispronounced and a confusion of words with similar sound patterns. We saw in Chapter 2 the typical phonological processes that young children experience; again, this underlines the importance of understanding the typical developmental pattern in order to spot something awry. One common way of measuring phonological processing is the non-word repetition task, which is what it sounds like! Children are asked to repeat nonsense words and those with SLI find this much harder, especially on words longer than three syllables (Brookes and Kempe, 2012: 221). It is generally held that this measures **phonological short-term memory** and this in turn can affect the acquisition of vocabulary. Of relevance to this is the difficulty that children with SLI may experience with selecting a target word from their vocabulary in the context of other words with similar sound patterns.

Another area that is affected in such children is phonological awareness (see Chapter 4). **Phonological awareness** is the ability to manipulate the sounds in words by such means as counting syllables, coming up with rhyming words and breaking down a word into its constituent parts. Children become aware of the larger units of speech first, such as syllables, often aided by familiar nursery rhymes or songs. They may show some creativity with this – one four-year-old we know, informed us that at a friend's house she had played on the 'vanana' – only when she told us it was black and white did the penny drop that she meant their piano, and had misheard the word. She then suddenly starting playing with the language, chanting 'vanana, vanana, lorryana, lorryana', showing that she was able to 'remove' the 'van' and replace it with 'lorry'! Only later do children develop **_phonemic_ awareness** – that is, explicit awareness of the phonemes of the language, such that they are able, for example, to say how many sounds there are in a word or replace one sound with another (Brookes and Kempe, 2012: 203). This ability plays a role in developing literacy skills, especially in an alphabetic writing system, and is why many believe that this should be taught explicitly to young children. This approach, commonly known as 'phonics', is seen by many as crucial (e.g. Stuart, 2006), although its precise role remains controversial for many (see Ellis and Moss, 2014).

LEXICAL PROCESSING

Problems with phonological short-term memory can in turn affect the acquisition of vocabulary and it is indeed the case that children with DLD have less varied receptive and expressive vocabularies than their peers. First words are delayed, words are learned more slowly and new words more quickly forgotten (see Brookes and Kempe, 2012: 223–4 for an overview). As Leonard notes (2015: 555–6), if children have limitations in phonological short-term memory, they may require more exposures to each new word before they can form an adequate phonological representation. This could slow the pace of lexical acquisition. Furthermore, children may find it harder to recall words, whether in conversation or in word-naming tasks, and this means that their conversation may seem stilted as they struggle to find the right words, pause, repeat themselves and use generic terms like 'thingy' whenever they cannot find the right vocabulary. Ratner (2001: 373) calls this 'general all-purpose' (GAP) nouns and verbs. She notes too that problems retrieving words can result in circumlocutions, citing the example of a child requesting 'something round and English' for his breakfast, failing to find the word 'muffin'. However, this is not just an issue of quantity (number of words in the lexicon). Children with DLD may have **semantic** problems – that is, problems with the meaning of words. They may name pictures more slowly than their peers and will often choose a word that is semantically related – although of course they may not know the vocabulary item (Ratner, 2001: 223). Other problems include difficulties in coming up with definitions of words, as theirs tend to be fewer and less accurate. And there appears to be greater difficulty acquiring verbs than nouns (Schwartz, 2009).

GRAMMATICAL DIFFICULTIES

According to Ratner (2001: 372), children with DLD tend to be identified not on the basis of their lexical performance, but by their failure to produce grammatical structures typical of their age, although this may or may not be accompanied by comprehension difficulties. We saw in Chapter 3 how important the development of grammatical morphology is. Ratner points out that their abilities to use grammatical morphemes and a range of simple and complex sentence structures are particularly depressed when compared to typically developing peers. Leonard notes that an especially well-documented problem in English-speaking children with SLI is a serious deficit in the use of grammatical morphemes that mark tense and agreement (2015: 546). Children with DLD learning English will experience problems with, for example, plurals, possessives, tense markers, articles, the verb *to be* and prepositions. And, of course, not all grammatical morphemes are equally salient in the stream of speech in the first place – for example, short unstressed syllables like the 'are' in 'are you coming?' or morphemes that aren't whole syllables (e.g. past tense –ed) .The most significant problems tend to be with verb inflections and agreement in the use of the verb *to be*, whether as a copula or an auxiliary. The term 'copula' refers to its use as a verb in its own right – for example, I am a teacher, she is nice and so on. The auxiliary *to be* is when it used to form the verb – for example, I am sitting, we were eating. Similarly, they experience problems with the auxiliary *do*, needed for the question system in English, as in *do you want a biscuit?* Interestingly, children tend to omit these rather than misuse or misplace them (Ratner, 2001). This might suggest that they have problems processing them and retaining them in short-term memory, as outlined above, underlining the complex interrelationship of different linguistic subsystems. Recall how the importance of these was stressed in Chapter 3: if children experience difficulties at this level, imagine how they will struggle with more complex constructions such as the modal auxiliaries as in: *would you have come if it had rained?* Needless to say, these problems with more advanced constructions as well as problems maintaining narrative coherence become more marked, with implications for school achievement (Ratner, 2001: 372). To understand narrative, children must learn to process sequences of utterances so that they form a coherent whole. Children who struggle with this may produce sequences of utterances that seem disconnected and hard to follow. They may also experience comprehension failure if they interpret one sentence at a time without drawing the necessary inferences to link them together (Karasinski and Weismer, 2010).

But are the children simply delayed? We saw in earlier chapters that there is indeed some variation among young children, making comparisons between children of comparable chronological ages difficult. Instead, a measure of mean length of utterance (MLU) is used, a long-established approach to measuring linguistic productivity in children proposed by Brown (1973). It is traditionally calculated by collecting 100 utterances spoken by a child and dividing the number of morphemes by the number of utterances. A higher **MLU** is taken to indicate a higher level of language proficiency. Children with SLI may reach a higher MLU before they acquire their first grammatical morphemes (Harris and Coltheart, 1986: 110). Studies have also shown that children with DLD matched for MLU with typically developing children tend to produce fewer grammatical morphemes, despite utterance length being the same (Steckol and Leonard, 1979; Leonard, 1995). This suggests that there may be more than delay going on.

In terms of comprehension, clearly if there are auditory processing problems such that children are missing parts of speech – or failing to commit them to short-term memory – this will affect their understanding of language. But at the level of syntax (sentence structure), there is some evidence that English-speaking children with SLI are less likely than their peers to rely upon word order to understand sentence structure, instead using lexical/semantic information. Some sentences are reversible, whereas others are not. So *the man chased the woman* is reversible, whereas *the girl ate the cake* is not. The former kind are much harder for children with SLI as they have to rely upon word order (*syntactic* information) to arrive at a correct interpretation, whereas *semantic* information (cakes don't eat girls) makes the second one easier to make sense of. Other complex sentence structures are passives (again some are reversible and others are not), wh– questions (*where did the man leave the shopping?*) and relative clauses (*the duck behind the cat was green*) (which one is green?). Even a simple sentence (SVO) can be difficult if each 'slot' has a long noun or verb phrase. *The rabbit ate the carrot* is much easier to process than *The big fat fluffy rabbit had been eating the delicious organic carrots*. But they are both simple sentences (see Chapter 2).

While observations of children with difficulties yield valuable findings, experimental studies also throw light upon their problems. Children with DLD struggle to repeat structures accurately and struggle in particular with negatives and questions – and when the sentence prompt gets longer. An early study by Menyuk (1978) highlighted the role of meaningfulness in the language processing of these children, as analysis of their attempts to repeat showed that they tried to preserve the meaning of the sentence rather than simply repeating the words they could remember.

A further consideration is the language children with DLD are learning. Languages differ in the importance they accord to, for example, word order. Languages vary too in the role that morphology plays. If we compare English and German, German has a very rich and complex morphology, whereas in English much meaning is conveyed by word order. This is further complicated by the fact that so many children grow up speaking more than one language (see Chapters 5 and 6), which points to the importance of children's language development being assessed in both or all languages.

To summarise thus far, then, children with DLD experience a range of difficulties in more than one domain. However, it remains to consider the domain of pragmatics, as the difficulties outlined above have inevitable implications for communication.

PRAGMATIC DIFFICULTIES

We have already seen the essential role that this plays in successful communication. Having read this chapter so far, it is probably not hard to imagine the challenges children with DLD face in **social interaction**, with teachers as well as with family and friends. We touched upon the requirements of conversation in the section on autism (see Chapter 7). To reiterate, we need to learn to initiate and maintain communication, take turns and be aware of our interlocutor. As Ninio and Snow point out, skilled conversationalists display rapid turn-taking, where each turn begins a microsecond before the previous one ends; they generally avoid periods of overlapping speech and interruptions; they are aware of when it is obligatory to respond – for example, failing to respond to a greeting is considered rude; moreover, they are aware of their obligations as a listener, showing attentiveness, indicating comprehension or lack of, and allowing the other speaker sufficient time and opportunity to speak; they have effective repair strategies when communication breaks down; and importantly they observe topic relevance, and are able to use explicit strategies for changing the topic, such as 'that reminds me' (Ninio and Snow, 1996: 144–6). We may underestimate the skill involved in relating one's utterance to the preceding one uttered by the other speaker and doing so appropriately, but this is essential to effective dialogue and different from early functions of speech – for example, requesting a drink. Unsurprisingly then, children with DLD will have difficulties initiating and sustaining social interaction because of the demands involved. Moreover, children do not simply converse in dialogue with one other – many conversations are group-based and children with SLI are known to struggle with joining established peer-group interactions. They may also fail to respond to communicative bids by other children (Brookes and Kempe, 2012: 226). Similarly, they may produce less appropriate requests or respond less appropriately to requests, and show less sensitivity to interlocutors' needs for clarification or information, or interpret language literally (Ratner, 2001: 373).

The impact of struggling in social interaction is not surprising; children may find they have difficulties socialising and feel isolated, even withdrawing from interaction. Lack of understanding on the part of other children or even bullying can have a distressing effect upon these children, particularly as, from pre-school age, children prefer to be friends with children with higher levels of communicative competence rather than lower (Barry *et al.*, 2007). Indeed, even by three or four years of age, children are aware of the communicative level of others, and prefer to interact with peers who have age-appropriate language skills (Bishop, 2003: 101). By pre-adolescence, studies have found lower levels of self-esteem which inevitably have a negative impact, with possible long-term repercussions.

A key issue here is whether pragmatic difficulties exist as a problem in their own right or arise from the problems that children are experiencing in the areas of phonology, grammar and lexicon. As Bishop (2003: 99–100) points out, there appear to be two kinds of reaction to these particular communication difficulties: on the one hand, there are those that argue that the difficulties in interaction arise as secondary to the structural language difficulties. As she says, if children struggle with speaking intelligibly, finding the right words or producing coherent speech, communication breaks down and people become reluctant to interact with the child, thus producing a vicious circle. On the other hand, she points to those who argue that a child displaying pragmatic difficulties should be considered as being on the autistic spectrum. Anyone with knowledge of autism (see Chapter 7) will have already spotted the similarities in the description of the communicative behaviours described here. As Bishop (2003) notes, given the social and behavioural problems that sometimes accompany the inappropriate use of language (that is otherwise well formed), some argue that this is not a *specific* impairment, but a pervasive developmental one (i.e. something broader). However, she urges caution in this regard, suggesting that we should not jump to conclusions, as children diagnosed with autism generally need to be seen to have the impairments associated with it. As we saw in Chapter 7, children with autistic spectrum conditions (ASC), while having social and communicative difficulties, also display other characteristics such as adherence to routine, dislike of change, repetitive patterns of behaviour and intense focus on particular topics or interests. Thus, we should be careful about assuming that a diagnosis of autism is appropriate. Bishop, however, concedes that there are some children whose pragmatic language impairment is difficult to explain because the child's use of language is disproportionately poor in relation to structural language, but concludes that there are many children who fall between the diagnostic options of SLI or autism: on the one hand, their developmental difficulties are not restricted to structural aspects of language, but, on the other, they do not have the full range of pervasive impairments that would warrant a diagnosis of autism (Bishop, 2003: 101). The difficulty in making an accurate diagnosis is compounded by the possibility that children who do not match 'clear-cut' examples of individuals with a disorder are often diagnosed differently by professionals with different types of training (e.g. psychiatrist versus speech and language therapist) (Botting and Conti-Ramsden, 2003: 515).

A further issue is that the profiles of children with SLI are also dynamic over time so that children who are identified as having a certain pattern of difficulties may improve in some areas and not in others, giving a different profile from year to year (Botting and Conti-Ramsden, 2004: 23).

Despite these difficulties of diagnosis, there would appear to be some children whose primary problem is a pragmatic one that may constitute a sub-group (van Balkom and Verhoeven, 2004: 283). Bishop (2003: 111–12), however, suggests that we may need to depict pragmatic language impairment (PLI) as literally intermediate between autism and SLI, rather than belonging with one or the other. In her view, what is crucial is looking carefully at pragmatics when assessing a child with language impairment and not automatically assuming that poor use of communication is a secondary symptom. Botting and Conti-Ramsden's (2003) study suggested, furthermore, that it may be possible to distinguish two groups – one they describe as 'PLI pure', characterised by severe pragmatic language difficulties without autistic traits (that is, lack of obsessive behaviour, rigidity of thought, or of marked social difficulties necessary for a diagnosis of autism, and the presence of significant linguistic difficulties not usually seen in those with what was then termed 'Asperger syndrome') and another they call 'PLI plus' who, as well as pragmatic language difficulties, appear to have some autistic-type characteristics.

To summarise thus far, for some children, learning to talk is not plain sailing. As we have seen, all aspects of language can be affected: phonological, lexical, grammatical and pragmatic and both comprehension (receptive) and production (expressive) of language can be impaired. The challenge in diagnosing and providing appropriate intervention for such children is that DLD is by no means homogeneous, presenting differently in different children – that is, a different combination of areas is affected. As already noted, a related and important issue that researchers have examined is whether language is simply delayed or is in fact different in some way. Hoff-Ginsberg (1997: 321–2) suggests a possible resolution to this, proposing that within each sub-system of language (phonology, grammar and so on) children with DLD may follow a typical developmental path, but with delay. However, she goes on to suggest that different sub-systems may be delayed to differing degrees, thus disrupting the usual synchrony seen in typically developing children and producing a pattern of language competencies not usually seen. However, this leaves us with the question: are there children who are simply delayed? And how do we know?

LATE TALKERS

We probably all know a parent who says their child did not talk early; those of us with experience of young children will no doubt have observed that they do indeed differ in the speed of acquisition, or of their clarity of expression. It is not uncommon to struggle to make out what very young children are saying and frequently they are understood by parents and other regular caregivers more readily than the occasional visitor. So what counts as talking late? We saw in Chapter 3 the typical developmental milestones. It appears that toddlers at 24 months who do not yet have an expressive vocabulary of 50 words and who do not produce any multi-word utterances (word combinations) are considered to be late talkers (Desmarais *et al.*, 2008). Late talkers are more likely to be boys than girls, and typically do not have the burst in vocabulary growth during the second year of life that characterises most typically developing children. Some late talkers do indeed catch up with their peers in the pre-school years, whereas others go on to attract a diagnosis of DLD. In terms of outcomes for late talkers, there may remain some subtle differences between such children and typically developing peers as there is some evidence that vocabulary 'recovers' more readily than syntactic and morphological development (Rescorla *et al.*, 1997). Can we predict which late talkers will 'bloom'? Some studies point to two things that may differentiate them: first, their *comprehension* of language; and, second, their use of gesture. The latter may be compensatory behaviour to facilitate social interaction with others (Capone and McGregor, 2004) and may be predictive of more positive longer-term outcomes. Indeed, we saw in Chapter 3 how important the non-linguistic element of communication is, particularly in using eye gaze, establishing joint attention and so on. It is thus not difficult to see how failure to develop these abilities would impact upon comprehension. Perhaps it is not surprising that these two features together are predictive of more successful outcomes.

WHAT EXPLANATIONS ARE THERE?

Parents and caregivers quite naturally will ask why this has occurred. Why has it? First, there does seem to be a genetic element to this, as language impairments tend to run in families (van der Wilt *et al.*, 2018). Some evidence for this comes from studies of twins, showing that the likelihood of both twins having SLI is significantly higher in identical twins than in fraternal twins (Tomblin, 2015). Of course, other factors can also play a part, such as prematurity, as babies born early have less positive language-learning outcomes than full-term babies (Vandormael *et al.*, 2019). While researchers have come up with various explanations, the main area of controversy is to do with the degree of language specificity there is. In other words, is the main issue a purely language-related one or is there a more general cognitive deficit that underlies it?

Linguistic explanations include the suggestion that children with DLD have deficits in what is called 'grammatical representation'. This means that they have difficulty inferring rules from the input so that the pattern of, for example, past tense endings is not intuited in the same way as it is by typically developing children. Proponents of this view contend that there is some innate grammatical component missing, although we should note that this assumes a degree of innateness to the grammar (see Chapter 1 on theories). A further linguistic explanation that we referred to above is that the role morphology plays in the particular language being learned may be a factor. Studies into other languages and of bilingual children are now beginning to shed more light on the language-specific difficulties that may exist (see, for example, Leonard, 2015).

Cognitive explanations, however, point to the possibility that processing deficits are the cause. We saw earlier in this chapter that children with SLI have long been known to have problems with auditory processing and it has been proposed that this lies at the core of SLI. Deficits in phonological memory have been proposed as children with SLI have been found to have difficulty with repeating sequences of unfamiliar sounds (Archibald and Gathercole, 2006). A somewhat broader explanation is the 'slowing hypothesis' which suggests that children with SLI have slower global cognitive processing, as measured by reaction times to various tasks (Schwartz, 2009: 9–10). Another explanation is that children with SLI have difficulty processing spoken language because they have limited verbal working memory capacity and find it tricky to process verbal information at the same time as other non-verbal information (Montgomery: 2000). This is related to the role of attention. As Archibald and Noonan (2015: 573) note, 'it is easy to imagine that the ability to focus, sustain and shift attention may play a key role in our ability to register and process incoming linguistic information'. They go on to review several studies to conclude that children with SLI perform more poorly than age-matched peers on tasks aimed at assessing attention with the deficits in sustained auditory attention being the most reliable. They caution, however, that a causal connection is by no means clear, suggesting that, although it is possible that attention deficits may contribute to impairments in language learning, it is equally possible that the presence of language impairments may constrain performance on many auditory attention tasks (2015: 574).

Others have proposed that the deficit may be in procedural memory. Procedural memory is a kind of long-term memory, a memory of how to *do* certain things. Much procedural learning is implicit – infants do not consciously learn how to walk, for example. Later on, skills such as swimming, riding a bike or typing may need a degree of instruction, but essentially the constant repetition of actions makes them automatic, so that we can do something without necessarily being able to explain how. This is different from declarative memory, which is when we intentionally remember something and can recall it – this is a distinction often used when thinking about learning a foreign language. We can memorise a verb table, for example, but being able to use the verbs procedurally requires a lot of practice before we produce them without thinking. Procedural memories form when connections are made between synapses in the brain and the more frequently an action is performed, the more often signals are sent through the same synapses. Over time, these synaptic routes become stronger and the actions themselves become automated and unconscious. How might this affect language development? Were this to be the case, it could impact upon motor skills and statistical learning of patterns and sequences, which could affect the ability to infer patterns in the linguistic input with the same ease as typically developing children.

As Brookes and Kempe point out (2012: 237), this hypothesis gains support from a broad literature documenting problems with motors skills and coordination in children with SLI. Some children with SLI have symptoms of dyspraxia, a motor-learning difficulty that can affect both gross and fine motor skills, perhaps appearing to be clumsy in their movements. This brings us to what is called 'co-morbidity', which is essentially the existence of more than one disorder in a person. We have seen throughout this chapter that not only are language disorders highly variable in their manifestations, but they are also difficult to pin down as discrete (dis)abilities with clear boundaries. On the contrary, they seem to co-exist or overlap with a number of other syndromes. For example, some children with SLI also have articulation disorders (Ratner, 2001: 373); other studies show co-morbidity of language impairments and attention deficits (Archibald and Noonan, 2015). Furthermore, there is a relatively high incidence of dyslexia and more global reading and writing problems (Schwartz, 2009: 3).

CHAPTER SUMMARY

This chapter has shown how for some children developing spoken language is not the easy path it is for many. The term 'developmental language disorder' is now the preferred description, and reflects the breadth and variety of the issues faced by some children, the possible overlap with other syndromes and the challenges this presents to researchers and practitioners alike. While numerous explanations have been offered, we as yet have no definitive one. What is clear, however, is that there is enormous diversity in the process of learning to talk, and it is imperative that an understanding of this informs the practice of all those who work with young children.

REFERENCES

Archibald, L.M.D. and Gathercole, S.E. (2006) Nonword repetition: a comparison of tests. *Journal of Speech, Language, and Hearing Research*, 49(5), 970–83.

Archibald, M.D. and Noonan, N.B. (2015) Processing deficits in children with language impairment. In E.L. Bavin and L.R. Naigles (eds), *Cambridge Handbook of Child Language*. 2nd edn. Cambridge: Cambridge University Press.

Barry J.G., Yasin I. and Bishop D.V. (2007) Heritable risk factors associated with language impairments. *Genes, Brain and Behavior*, 6, 66–76.

Bishop, D.V.M. (2003) Pragmatic language impairment: a correlate of SLI, a distinct subgroup, or part of the autistic continuum? In D.V.M. Bishop and L.B. Leonard (eds), *Speech and Language Impairments in Children: Causes Characteristics, Intervention, and Outcome*. Hove: Psychology Press.

Bishop, D.V.M., Snowling, M.J., Thompson, P.A., Greenhalgh, T. and the CATALISE 656 Consortium (2016) CATALISE: a multinational and multidisciplinary Delphi 657 consensus study: identifying language impairments in children. *PLOS One*, 11(7), 658 e0158753. doi:doi:10.1371/journal.pone.0158753

Bishop, D.V.M. , Snowling, M.J., Thompson, P.A. , Greenhalgh T. and the CATALISE-2 Consortium (2017) Phase 2 of CATALISE: a multinational and multidisciplinary Delphi consensus study of problems with language development: terminology. *Journal of Child Psychology and Psychiatry*, 58(10), 1068–80.

Botting, N. and Conti-Ramsden, G. (2003) Autism, primary pragmatic difficulties, and specific language impairment: can we distinguish them using psycholinguistic markers? *Developmental Medicine and Child Neurology*, 45: 515–24.

Botting, N. and Conti-Ramsden, G. (2004) Characteristics of children with specific language impairment. In L. Verhoeven and H. van Balkom (eds), *Classification of Developmental Language Disorders: Theoretical Issues and Clinical Implications*. Mahwah, NJ, and London: Lawrence Erlbaum.

Brookes, P.J. and Kempe, V. (2012) *Language Development*. Oxford: Blackwell.

Brown, R. (1973) *A First Language: The Early Stages*. Harmondsworth: Penguin.

Capone, N.C. and McGregor, K.K. (2004) Gesture development: a review for clinical and research practices. *Journal of Speech and Hearing Research*, 47, 173–86.

Corriveau, K., Pasquini, E. and Goswami, U. (2007) Basic auditory processing skills and specific language impairment: a new look at an old hypothesis. *Journal of Speech, Language, and Hearing Research*, 50(3), 647–66.

Desmarais, C., Sylvestre, A., Meyer, F., Baraiti, I. and Rouleau, N. (2008) Systematic review of the literature on characteristics of late-talking toddlers. *International Journal of Communication Disorders*, 43, 361–89.

Ellis, S. and Moss, G. (2014) Ethics, education policy and research: the phonics question reconsidered. *British Educational Research Journal*, 40(2), 241–60.

Harris, M. and Coltheart, M. (1986) *Language Processing in Children and Adults: An Introduction*. London: Routledge and Kegan Paul.

Hoff-Ginsberg, E. (1997) *Language Development*. Pacific Grove, CA: Brooks/Cole.

Karasinski, C. and Weismer, S.E. (2010) Comprehension of inferences in discourse processing by adolescents with and without language impairment. *Journal of Speech, Language and Hearing Research*, 53(5), 1268–79.

Leonard, L.B. (1995) Functional categories in the grammar of children with specific language impairment. *Journal of Speech and Hearing Research*, 38, 1270–83.

Leonard, L.B. (2015) Language symptoms and their possible sources of specific language impairment. In E.L. Bavin and L.R. Naigles (eds), *Cambridge Handbook of Child Language*. 2nd edn. Cambridge: Cambridge University Press.

Menyuk, P. (1978) Linguistic problems in children with developmental dysphasia. In M. Wyke (ed.), *Developmental Dysphasia*. London: Academic Press.

Montgomery, J.W. (2000) Verbal working memory and sentence comprehension in children with specific language impairment. *Journal of Speech and Hearing Research*, 43, 293–308.

Ninio, A. and Snow, C.E. (1996) *Pragmatic Development*. Boulder, CT: Westview Press.

Ratner, N.B. (2001) Atypical language development. In J.B. Gleason (ed.), *The Development of Language*. 5th edn. London: Allyn & Bacon.

Rescorla, L. Roberts, J. and Dahlsgaard, K. (1997) Late talkers at 2: outcome at age 3. *Journal of Speech and Hearing Research*, 40, 556–66.

Schwartz, R.G. (2009) Specific language impairment. In R.G. Schwartz (ed.), *Handbook of Child Language Disorders*. New York: Psychology Press.

Steckol, K.F. and Leonard, L.B. (1979) The use of grammatical morphemes by normal and language-disordered children. *Journal of Communication Disorders*, 12, 291–301.

Stuart, M. (2006) Learning to read the words on the page: the crucial role of early phonics teaching. In M. Lewis and S. Ellis (eds), *Phonics: Practice, Research and Policy*. London: Paul Chapman.

Tallal, P. and Piercy, M. (1973) Defects of nonverbal auditory perception in children with developmental aphasia. *Nature*, 241, 468–9.

Tomblin, J.B. (2015) Children with specific language impairment (SLI). In E.L. Bavin and L.R. Naigles (eds), *Cambridge Handbook of Child Language*. 2nd edn. Cambridge: Cambridge University Press.

Tomblin, J.B., Records, N.L., Buckwalter, P.R., Zhang, X., Smith, E. and O'Brien, M. (1997) Prevalence of specific language impairment in kindergarten children. *Journal of Speech, Language, and Hearing Research*, 40, 1245–60.

van Balkom, H. and Verhoeven, L. (2004) Pragmatic disability in children with specific language impairments. In L. Verhoeven and H. van Balkom (eds), *Classification of Developmental Language Disorders: Theoretical Issues and Clinical Implications*. Mahwah, NJ, and London: Lawrence Erlbaum.

van der Wilt, F., van der Veen, C., van Kruistum, C. and van Oers, B. (2018) Popular, neglected, rejected, controversial, or average: do young children from different sociometric groups differ in their level of oral communicative competence? *Social Development*, 27, 793–807.

Vandormael, C., Schoenhals, L., Hüppi, P.S., Filippa, M. and Tolsa, C.B. (2019) Language in preterm born children: atypical development and effects of early interventions on neuroplasticity (Hindawi). *Neural Plasticity*, Article ID 6873270, 1–10. Available at: https://doi.org/10.1155/2019/6873270

APPENDIX I

In the chart below, you can see that the place of articulation is across the top, with the bilabial on the left and the glottal on the right. If you look again at the diagram of speech organs (Fig.2.1 on p.24), you will see that, like the diagram, we go left to right from the front to the back of the mouth. Down the left hand side you'll see that the manner of articulation is noted. You should also note that it is a convention to write the voiceless sound on the left and the voiced on the right on phonemic alphabet charts.

Now take a look at the following chart:

	Bi–labial		Labio–dental		Dental		Alveolar		Palate–alveolar		Palatal		Velar		Glottal	
Voiced/unvoiced	−v	+v	−v	+v	−v	+v	−v	+v	−v	+v	−v	+v	−v	+v	−v	+v
Plosives	p	b					t	d					k	g		
Fricatives			f	v	θ	ð	s	z	ʃ	ʒ					h	
Affricates									tʃ	dʒ						
Nasals	m							n						ŋ		
Laterals								l								
Approximants	w							r				j				

What sounds do the symbols represent?

This group represents the sounds you would expect: p b t d k g f v s z h l w r l

NOTE that the symbol /j/ represents the 'y' sounds in e.g. ' yacht' or 'young'

The unfamiliar looking symbols represent sounds as follows:

θ = **th**in

ð = **th**e

ʃ = **sh**ip

ʒ = vi**s**ion

tʃ = **ch**icken

dʒ = **j**am

ŋ = ha**ng**

Here are some examples of how the symbols represent the orthography of English:

p	b	t	d	tʃ	dʒ	k	g
pig	big	time	day	chicken	jam	kill	got
f	v	θ	ð	s	z	ʃ	ʒ
five	vase	thin	then	sit	zoo	ship	vision
m	n	ŋ	h	l	r	w	j
man	no	hang	hat	last	run	wish	yacht

APPENDIX II

The diagram below represents the place in the mouth where the monopthongs are produced. You can see, for example, that /i:/ (as in 'been') is high in the mouth and at the front, whereas /a:/ (as in 'bar') is at the back of the mouth and low down.

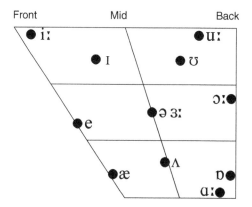

Image from: https://commons.wikimedia.org/wiki/File:RP_vowel_chart_(monophthongs).gif

Here are some examples of how the symbols represent the orthography of English, with the dipthongs in bold:

ɪ	iː	ʊ	uː	ɪə	eɪ	
bin	been	pull	glue	**here**	**day**	
e	ə	ɜː	ɔː	ʊə	ɔɪ	əʊ
bed	about	shirt	sort	**tour**	**boy**	**go**
æ	ʌ	ɑː	ɒ	eə	aɪ	aʊ
cat	but	bar	cot	**pear**	**my**	**now**

INDEX